The World is a
Narrow Bridge

Stories that Celebrate Hope and Healing

With an introduction by Craig Taubman

Edited by
Diane Arieff

All Rights Reserved under International and Pan American copyright conventions. © 2004 Sweet Louise Productions. *The World is a Narrow Bridge* was made possible by the Ziegler Family Foundation, and with the guidance and support of Synagogue 2000, HUC-JIR Kalsman Institute of Judaism and Health, and The National Center for Jewish Healing.

ISBN 1-886926-11-5

The world is a narrow bridge.
The key to the crossing is not to be afraid.
-Rabbi Nachman of Bratzlav

Introduction

The idea was simple. Collect twelve songs and twelve essays that would comfort and inspire people who are dealing with illness or loss. Two years and four months later, I can assure you that the process of bringing that idea to fruition has been anything but simple. Along the way, I've learned that book projects don't always proceed as planned. In the same way that an illness or a loss disrupts our lives and throws a wrench into careful plans, on a smaller scale, seeing this book through has meant dealing with the inevitable bumps in the road and learning to surmount the unexpected hurdles.

Happily, I think the delays and the extra effort were well worth the wait. The twelve original essays grew to fifty. People came out of the woodwork to contribute. Many of them ended up sharing very personal stories, with the hope that others would gain strength from reading about their experiences.

These essays cover a wide range of subject matter and every sort of mood, from lighthearted to somber. Some are written as poems. Others are personal prayers. Some are recollections, and others are interpretations of text. It's as if fifty different roads were taken. Yet each traveler is on the same essential journey – from darkness to light, from pain to peace, from loss to hope, from grief to healing.

On some level, each of these essays addresses the task of embracing the lives that we are given, in all their messy bittersweetness. Where can we find comfort? Solace? What will be the first step on the road to healing? How do we begin? The answers change from year to year, from person to person. Some find spiritual healing in music. For others, the poetic imagination is a necessary refuge. We find healing in our connections to loved ones and in our encounters with strangers. We find it in ritual, in prayer, and in the ongoing loop of our own memories. We find healing in new experiences, in doing good deeds, in discovering new perspectives. We find healing in letting go and in the simple passage of time.

It's my hope that in these pages you'll find some spark, some measure of inspiration and comfort. Use this book. Share it with friends and family, with people who are coping with illness or other sorts of loss. Read these stories out loud. Talk about them at your Shabbat table. You might even consider including a story from the book or a song from the companion CD as part of a funeral service, a memorial, during a Shiva, or as a Kavanah/introspection before reciting the Mourner's Kaddish. Write your own thoughts in the margins. Send us your reactions, your ideas and stories…. Who knows, there might turn out to be a "Volume II."

In Pirkei Avot, Rabbi Hillel says, "Do not separate yourself from the community." I know firsthand that this book would never have been possible without a community of family, friends and colleagues who were instrumental in making this project a reality. I extend my thanks to Ruth Ziegler, Ron Wolfson, Lisa Kodmur, Randee Friedman, Steve Silberman, Howard Cooper, Mark Kligman, Judah Cohen, Simkha Y. Weintraub, Melanie Fisher, Debbie Miller, Beth Goldsmith and, of course, Louise Taubman. A special thank you to Danny Kodmur for helping me assemble these pieces for the initial edit and to Mike Cardinal, friend and graphic artist extraordinaire. To Pam Kaizer and Julie Kinrich for proofreading every word, letter and em dash. To Etan Milgrom, my heartfelt thanks, not only for being a good friend, but for planting the seed that led to the creation of this project. Finally, I owe a huge debt of gratitude to Diane Arieff, who took a bunch of wonderful essays and magically made them come together as a beautiful book.

– Craig Taubman

Table of Contents

Love & Community:
Connection to Others

Just as despair can come to one another only from other human beings,
hope, too, can be given to one only by other human beings.

– *Elie Wiesel*

Dreams that Vanish—and Don't

Leonard Fein

Soon after my daughter Nomi died—suddenly, at age 30, of cardiac arrest—I wrote an article thanking the many people who'd reached out in friendship and consolation. I called the piece, "As A Dream That Vanishes," the closing words of the *U'Ntaneh Tokef*, the immensely central High Holiday prayer that speaks of God as the one who decides who shall live and who shall die, who by fire, who by plague, and so forth—and who, most important to me, "in the fullness of time, who before his time."

My brief article included an excerpt from a remarkable letter Nomi had written just before her 13th birthday, a letter filled with hope and reverence.

Weeks later, I received a letter from a rabbi in Tucson, a Conservative rabbi whom I did not know. He'd read my article, and was moved to challenge me: "This dream will not vanish," he wrote. And went on to cite what he described as "the well-known Talmudic dictum"—I always tremble when people say such things, since so often they are not "well-known" to me—*gvilin nisrafin v'ha'otiyot porchot ba'avir*, which translates as "the parchment is consumed, and" (or "but," if you will) "the letters blossom in the air."

The "dictum" comes from the Martyrology. Within the Yom Kippur Musaf service, a section describes the death of ten martyrs at the hands of the Romans. One of the ten was Rabbi Chananya ben Tradion. The Midrash teaches that he was executed on the pretext of teaching Torah publicly, a capital offense according to Roman law. The Romans wrapped his Torah scroll around him, having packed his chest with wool soaked in water to prolong his agony, and set him on fire. When his disciples called out to him, he responded: "The parchment is consumed, but the letters fly up in the air."

Those words were immensely helpful to me, and all the more comforting since they came almost by accident, from a stranger. They are now, in fact, engraved on Nomi's headstone. Whether they mean so much because they are at least somewhat true, or because they remind me how meaningful, in all its modest kindness, the rabbi's letter truly was, I cannot say—nor does it matter. In the face of the death of a loved one, we feel our desperate, profound existential alone-ness. The embrace of others—friends and also kind strangers—saves us from descending forever into that darkness. It lets us pretend—it is only a pretense, after all—that we are not alone. It is almost physical, as if we are being grabbed, pulled back from the brink. As cold as we have been left and colder still as we sense we're becoming, the kindness of others acts as a blanket, enveloping us in warmth, restoring us to life.

Leonard Fein is a teacher, writer, and social activist. He is the founder of *Moment* magazine, as well as of the National Jewish Coalition for Literacy and Mazon: A Jewish Response to Hunger, which has disbursed more than $35 million to soup kitchens, food banks and other organizations since its founding in 1985. Fein's most recent book is *Against the Dying of the Light: A Father's Story of Love, Loss and Hope* (Jewish Lights Publishing, 2003).

Attaboy!

Danny Kodmur

I.   Dodger Stadium, circa 1979. The game is over, and I slowly make my way up the stairs from our seats, my crutches providing the means to get me from there to the gallery where my wheelchair lies parked, waiting.

The stone steps, narrow, unpredictable, messy with food, are an obstacle to be traversed slowly, carefully. As I approach a row of seats, random people start calling out encouragement: "Attaboy, you're doin' great! Keep at it! Good job!" Outwardly, I smile and thank them, maybe cracking wise that my crutches make me part-mountain-goat. Inwardly, I want to scream, "The game's over! Haven't you guys watched enough for one afternoon? Leave me alone, get out of my face, and let me focus on what I'm doing, so I don't fall on my tush!" I'd rather they ignored me, but I know damn well they won't, so I figure, why not give them a good show, take their minds off the Heroic Spectacle of the Crippled Boy on the Stairs? It doesn't mean I have to like it….

II.   A Fairfax District Jewish convalescent hospital, a few years earlier. I am there to see my frail, devout, and reclusive grandma, and to show her the latest skill in my arsenal, walking with crutches. She kvells as expected, but a nearby old lady becomes agitated: "De boy iz sufferink! De boy iz sufferink!"

How do I tell her it's no big deal, penetrate her anguished tsk-tsk-ing?

How do I handle the sincere Christian strangers who touch me on the street, telling me Jesus can heal me? I smile and say, "God bless you, too!" hoping for a hasty yet graceful exit.

III.   One day at school, someone I'd thought of as a friend says to me: "Man, I don't know how you do it. I think if I had a disability, I'd kill myself!" I resist the urge to scream and pummel him mercilessly, but honestly, adolescence is hard enough. This kind of talk I don't need. At all. Ever.

IV.   I hate to admit it, but maybe he's onto something. Whether people see me as plucky, heroic, or tragic, they are assuming I do what they could not: contend with the impossible. Whether in pity or admiration, they proceed from the premise that life with a disability is an endless war, a painful struggle, an endurance of the unendurable. If I told them how rarely not being able to walk crosses my mind, would anyone believe me?

V.   My life is not a re-enactment of the Chanukah revolt against tyranny, nor despite my name is it an endless loop of Daniel in the lion's den. It's just simply my reality. Calling it a triumph or a tragedy is misguided; those terms are outsider's language, an effort to impose a meaningful narrative arc on me, to slap on a cheap label while leaving ample room for the assumptions and fears my presence can inspire. In such circumstances, I end up feeling like the main character in a daytime soap I can't even watch.

VI.   If you really want to know me, don't stand outside worrying, assuming, pointing. Come inside my life. Sit with me. Ask anything you want, even if it's a question I'm sick of. Cry or laugh with me, but don't label my life. I won't label yours. I can't. I don't know enough about you.
       My disability is tough to gauge: sometimes hours can go by without my ever thinking about it, while at other times I end up obsessing over its impact and ramifications until my brain is fried. I do know it's a reality that's shaped who I am; like my Jewish identity, my disabled self is too complex to be covered in 750 words or less, too rich and confusing for someone else to categorize.

VII.   For me, being disabled isn't about a macho "Attaboy!" ability to overcome adversity or a resigned, tragic "sufferink." It's about maneuvering and negotiating, learning, arguing, exploring, challenging limits, and participating in an ongoing, evolving relationship. Maybe my disability is like an especially stimulating chunk of Talmud, with permanent boisterous study sessions attached. Want to join the class? Come on in; it's not at all what you'd expect. Trust me.

A native of Los Angeles, Danny Kodmur holds degrees in history from Stanford and UC Berkeley. He writes a regular column for the webzine *BENT* (www.bentvoices.org) and helped assemble the essays for this book. He lives in Berkeley, California.

Care Giving

Ron Wolfson

Joe Rothkop had broken his leg in a major car accident. While recuperating at a Los Angeles area rehabilitation facility, he met Boysie Sarmiento, a young nurse assistant working in the physical therapy clinic. The two men bonded instantly, sharing a story of caring and healing, giving and receiving, learning and love.

No two people could have been more dissimilar: Joe, a tall, handsome, nearly ninety-year-old man who hailed from Omaha, Nebraska, and Boysie, a diminutive, wispy twenty-year-old immigrant from the Philippines, brought together by the need for healing, they were patient and care giver. Having to provide care in the often-stifling rehab center was challenging and frustrating, but Joe, his wife, and their daughters noticed that Boysie never seemed fazed by anything. If he was embarrassed or sickened by the tasks he was asked to do, he never let on. He approached each day and each interaction with a smile and an attitude that flowed from some deep reservoir of human compassion. Joe responded to this with his own wonderful warmth.

When Joe was finally ready to return to his West Los Angeles home, the family asked Boysie if he was interested in becoming Joe's full-time care giver. Boysie had only recently graduated his nurse's assistant program, and had never taken on this kind of responsibility. However, out of a fondness for Joe nurtured through the months of rehabilitation, he agreed to take the job.

My family has been close to the Rothkops for more than seventy years, so when Joe and Harriet moved to California from Omaha a dozen years ago, Susie and I included them in many of our family functions and, of course, the Rothkops reciprocated. When Joe's health made it difficult for him to go out, we would visit and witness firsthand the extraordinary relationship between Joe and Boysie.

Most of the time, they would giggle. Two men giggling–over inside jokes, funny situations, and Joe's attempts at humor. Joe loved a good story and loved repeating them even more; Boysie laughed and laughed, no matter how many times he'd heard them. Proud of Boysie's steadily improving English, Joe would sometimes ask him to tell these stories himself.

Boysie's English wasn't the only language that was improving. Joe also set about teaching him Yiddish and Yiddishkeit. Joe wasn't very religious, but he loved being Jewish. One day, while

Boysie wheeled him out the front door, Joe noticed a five-pound box of matzah on the hallway table. "What's that?" Joe asked Boysie. "Oh, that's our matzahs, Joe," Boysie matter-of-factly responded. We once visited Joe on a Friday evening, and Boysie welcomed us at the front door. "Shabbat Shalom!" he exclaimed.

The affection between Joe and Boysie was palpable. Joe was like a father to him, encouraging his studies and his dreams, the strongest of which was his desire to become an American citizen. When Boysie passed his exam and got his papers, Joe was back at another rehab center, but he and his family still arranged a huge party to celebrate Boysie's accomplishment, complete with Uncle Sam hats for the nurses, Sousa marches, and an enormous cake.

Joe's wife, Harriet, recalls that no matter how difficult it was to take care of Joe, Boysie always had a smile and a warm word. Caring for more than just Joe's physical condition, he listened and learned as Joe taught him life lessons, enabling Joe to be a teacher, a mentor, a guide. In a way, they were care givers for each other.

As the end came, Joe was surrounded by his family, his friends, and Boysie. We were each privileged to say our good-byes to him, to hold his hand, to kiss his forehead, to let him go. When it was Boysie's turn, he caressed Joe's face and his eyes filled with tears. He said simply, *Gay shlofen*, Joe.

At Joe's funeral, his wife, daughters, and son-in-law shared expressions of love and warmth with all those who knew him, but perhaps the most heartfelt thanks were offered to Boysie, for giving care and dignity, laughter and love to their beloved husband and father.

Toward those unusual human beings who are the true healers in our midst, we can feel nothing except the deepest and most profound gratitude for the gifts they give us.

Dr. Ron Wolfson is a Vice President and Dean of the Fingerhut School of Education, University of Judaism. He is the author of *Shabbat, Passover, Hanukkah* and *A Time to Mourn, A Time to Comfort* (Jewish Lights).

Daily Loss

Carin Davis

I curl up on the couch with a box of Franzia wine and a gallon of ice cream. Full-fat ice cream. Like Job in high heels, I've watched my life unravel over the past two weeks. I lost my job, I lost my man, I lost my car in the Westfield Mall parking lot. The only thing I didn't lose was those last five pounds. Nobody knows the tsuris I've seen.

When the crises first hit, I threw on lip-gloss and a happy face and told everyone I'd be fine, that it would all be okay. Optimism–don't leave home without it. But two weeks later, this Pollyanna can't leave the couch, let alone home. I know break-ups and layoffs are some of the chutes and ladders of daily life. They're not world-shattering problems, but they sure shattered my world.

I try to watch a DVD, but even my Blockbuster night bugs. In real life, girls don't get the perfect job, the charming guy, and the "It was always you, kid," speech. We get bald blind dates. We get a table for one. We get a red, swollen nose from crying for two weeks straight into "aloe inside" tissues that claim to prevent the same Rudolphian symptoms I now endure.

Why? Why is this happening to me? I'm a good person. I call my parents, I keep kosher, I lead an honest life. Okay, fine, not totally honest–I've swiped hotel lotion from the maid's cart and I cheated on the Atkins diet. But even those of us who commit such brazen acts deserve happiness.

I ditch my fetal position and check out the self-help section at the late night Borders' Books. I pick up Everything Seems Better in the Morning, Everything Seems Better after a Second Helping of Dessert, and an annoyingly optimistic quote-of-the-day calendar. Of course these authors are optimistic; they each have a two-book publishing deal, an Oprah appearance on their resume and an aisle display at the bookstore. What do they know from problems? I try to re-shelve the books, but at 5'2", I'm too short to do it without a struggle. Like the walls of Jericho, the shelves come tumblin' down. Books flying, arms flailing, people staring, and my Kleenex blizzarding everywhere. All I can do is laugh. At that moment, for the first time in weeks, I feel okay.

At twenty-nine years old, I find that it's the ordinary things that lead to the dark, lonely times when I feel like I can't breathe. It's life's everyday losses that add up. But I know the greatest loss would be the loss of hope, so I hold on. I lean on my friends and family, and I remind myself to laugh. I also remind myself that things could always be worse. I could be thirty.

Carin Davis is a "Singles" columnist for *The Jewish Journal of Greater Los Angeles*. Always looking for the humor in life, her essays capture the comedy of kosher kissing, single-girl adventures, and dating disasters.

Opening a Door
Ed Feinstein

On Highway 101, about an hour south of San Francisco, stands a remarkable spiritual landmark. For years we drove up the coast and saw signs enticing us to see "The Winchester Mystery House." One year, we finally stopped to visit.

Sarah Winchester had married into the Winchester Rifle family. When both her husband and child died suddenly, she became convinced that the family was cursed by the spirits of all those who had been murdered by Winchester Rifles. Told by a well-known psychic that the only way to escape these angry spirits was to go west, buy a house and never stop building it, Mrs. Winchester abandoned her comfortable life in Connecticut, moved to the California wilderness town of Santa Clara, purchased a six-room farmhouse and began a fifty-year project of obsessive construction and reconstruction. At one time the house contained over 300 rooms, with staircases that led to nowhere, closets inside of closets, and bizarre rooms of every shape and dimension.

The mistress of her bizarre mansion, Mrs. Winchester never invited anyone in. She spoke only to a servant and her builder. Her plan successful, she eluded death until her 80's. She also eluded life.

The Winchester House, an odd, architectural monument to eccentricity, is a poignant reminder of how grief and fear can trap a human soul. Poor Mrs. Winchester stayed locked inside her ever-expanding house, while her ever-growing pain, her ever-deepening sorrow, turned more grotesque and bizarre with each new cycle of fanatical construction.

Ironically, during the years of her compulsion, a community grew up around her home. If only she had once opened the front door and invited the neighbors in for tea, letting their children fill the miles of hallways with laughter and play. If only Mrs. Winchester had believed she was not alone in this world.

As I walked through that strange house, I realized I know Mrs. Winchester–I am Mrs. Winchester. In my fortieth year, I was treated for colon cancer. Four years later, the cancer returned in a much more vicious form. The hardest part was not the surgery, the chemotherapy, the fatigue or the fear, but talking about it with my wife and children–acknowledging that our lives had changed. I couldn't share the struggle. I remember rehearsing my resolution: "I have spent a lifetime learning to be strong, I'm not going to change now."   "I solve problems for a living, I'll handle this."   "My job in life is to protect my family." So I remained stoic and silent...locked in my own Mystery House.

As I built this edifice of stoic fortitude with its endless network of catwalks and trapdoors, I was blind to the fact that the cancer had spread, metastasizing to my wife and my children, to my family and friends. My resolution didn't shield them. On the contrary, because of my stoicism, they suffered more. Cancer infects the whole family, the whole community. It poisons our hopes, contaminates our dreams, steals our tomorrows. My isolation, in the lonely garrets of stubborn masculine self-sufficiency, deprived others who wanted and needed to help me.

Pity Mrs. Winchester and all who cannot ask for help; we can help each other heal, but doing so means coming down from the attic; from the place of false heroism, from obstinate self-posses-sion. It means opening the front door and letting others in. The Lubavitcher Rebbe taught that God constantly rains blessings of healing down on the earth. The problem is that not everyone owns a bucket. Not everyone is ready to accept and gather the blessing.

Healing means accepting the blessings of life, moving from despair to affirmation, from denial to acceptance to celebration. In healing, we learn to endure–to withstand the loss, and still fill life with meaning. Even in the face of death, we can affirm life; we can share blessings. Traditionally, Jews pray for *refuah shelayma*, "a healing of wholeness." We do not seek a life without suffering–that is not the human condition. We pray for the wisdom and courage to embrace life in the very midst of death.

"I have set before you life and death, blessing and curse. Choose life." This is the most difficult mitzvah in the Torah. It is also the most important.

Ed Feinstein is rabbi of Valley Beth Shalom in Encino, CA, and the author of *Tough Questions Jews Ask – A Young Adult's Guide to Building a Jewish Life* (Jewish Light, 2003). Ed is a cancer patient and still bakes brownies every Friday from a recipe given his ancestors at Mt. Sinai.

The Wholeness of a Broken Heart

Neshama Carlebach

My father, Shlomo Carlebach, was my best friend, my inspiration, my Rebbe, my connection to G-d. He was everything to me. He traveled so much that I sometimes saw him only a few days a month, but we spoke many times a day. I remember being eight years old and sneaking out of class to use his calling card in order to phone him in Australia before a concert. No matter where he was, I could always reach him. If he was in a different time zone and it meant that I called him in the middle of the night, he would say, "My sweetest love, thank you so much for waking me up." He knew my heart. He knew all my stories. He 'got me'; I loved him so much.

When he died in 1994, it felt like my world had stopped spinning. He was coming to be with us for Shabbos, a rare and treasured event. I went to the airport to meet him, but instead of running into his arms, I found crying passengers telling me he was sick and had been taken off the plane in New York.

My best friend was suddenly gone, and I knew nothing would ever be the same. I would never be the same.

In his absence, I found myself traveling to sing his songs–a comfort to all the people who had been touched by him and so affected by his death. Many times, they couldn't stop crying. "He's still alive," I would say in concerts. "He is with us more than ever." But I didn't really believe it.

My father had always said a broken heart is the most whole. It's only after we are ripped apart that we can taste and understand what pure joy is. In an interview, when asked what the most joyous moment of his life was, he said "When my daughter Neshamale was born." "What did you do?" they asked, and he said, "I was up all night crying and praying to G-d that I would be at her wedding." This absolutely devastated me. I thought constantly of all he would be missing. It even crossed my mind that when I would marry, the wedding should have to be at his grave so he would be there.

My mother, Neila, who seemed to keep the world together with her bare hands, was once asked "What do you do with the hole in your heart?" She said, "It's always there, but I have planted flowers around it." That statement changed me. I went searching for flowers to plant next to the cemetery that was in my soul.

It was a long journey. It took me almost nine years before I could taste the joy my father described. I had known what it was to be broken. After so much sadness, my sister Dari and I were married within two months of each other.

From the moment I met Steven, I knew he'd be my healing. He taught me how to smile again. Like my sister's husband, Ari, Steven never had a chance to know my father. But both of them brought our father back to us in ways we never expected.

Dari's wedding was incredible. I was sure my father's presence would be there strongly that day, but I had no idea the impact it would have on me. My mother and I walked Dari down the aisle. Although I was standing in my father's place, my feet never touched the ground. He carried us all to her chuppah. That day, it was clear to me that heaven and earth were united.

The night before my own wedding, I was up all night praying that my father would also be there. I was crying as I hadn't in years, begging G-d to let him share my highest time with me. I walked down the aisle towards Steven, my soulmate, accompanied halfway by my mother and sister. Then I continued walking alone. Only, I wasn't alone. I knew with every part of my being that I was truly holding my father's hand. And it was just as my father always said: my broken heart was finally whole. I never knew that such joy could exist.

Neshama Carlebach is following in the tradition of soul singing and storytelling established by her father, the beloved Rabbi Shlomo Carlebach, an irrepressible spirit and composer of *niggunim* who was once described as the "Pied Piper of Judaism." Neshama's talent and charisma onstage have endeared her to people of all ages as she entertains and inspires in cities around the world, performing her own compositions as well as her father's classics. Her website is www.neshamacarlebach.com.

Healing & Heroism
Steven Carr Reuben

It was watching that lovely sixteen-year-old with a walker, both legs in bandages and struggling to take a few painful steps down the hallway of the hospital in Tel Aviv that got to me first. There I was, on the first of four intense days in Israel with a "Fact-Finding Solidarity Mission" of lay leaders from the Jewish Federation of Los Angeles, watching her courage and trying to hold back the tears. We were visiting at the time with nine remarkably brave teenagers who had survived the horrific terrorist suicide bombing just one month earlier at The Dolphenarium, a Tel Aviv beachfront disco popular with teenagers.

Twenty-one laughing, bubbly teenagers died that night in the bombing, and scores more were wounded. These nine with whom we were visiting were the ones still left in the hospital, slogging through each day of physical therapy and wondering how to cope with the lifelong emotional scars of that traumatic night. Every one was a recent immigrant from Russia, and every one had a best friend who died that night at the discotheque.

Perhaps the greatest irony of all was that everywhere we went in Israel, without exception, everyone we met greeted us with overwhelming gratitude, showering us with praise "for being brave enough to come and be with us." From cab drivers to the President of Tel Aviv University, from the mayor of Tel Aviv to the Prime Minister of Israel, every single person kept telling us that we were courageous, that we were brave.

But each of us knew the truth. Each of us shook our heads, looked at the empty shopping malls and tourist hotels and knew that they, the ones who lived there every day, holding up the torch of Jewish civilization in the ancient land of its birth, they were the brave ones, they were the ones with courage. All we did was visit for a few days and leave.

Talking with those kids and hearing them thank us for coming to see them set the tone for our entire trip. In broken English, one especially sweet young girl thanked me for bringing them the message that Jews all over the world hurt with them, care about them, cry for every child senselessly murdered or maimed, and ache for all the childhoods that have been stolen away.

I couldn't hold back my own tears then, or at other times in those four packed days; every time we met with other high school children, we heard them speak of their dreams for peace, of wanting to make a difference in the world. In the end I learned a valuable lesson about healing and heroism: sometimes the most powerful thing you can do is also the simplest. The most important thing any of us can do for those we love, those in need of healing, those who suffer, is simply to show up. Sometimes just being fully present for another human being can truly be the greatest gift of all.

Rabbi Steven Carr Reuben, Ph.D., is Senior Rabbi of Kehillat Israel Reconstructionist Congregation in Pacific Palisades, California, and the author of *Children of Character: Leading Your Children to Ethical Choices in Everyday Life* (Canter & Associates, 1997).

Healing and Hope
Selma R. Schimmel

As a two-time cancer survivor, of breast cancer at 28 and ovarian cancer at 48, I have had a lot of opportunity to ponder healing and hope. There are many aspects of life over which we lack control; it's how we interpret and work with and through life's most difficult encounters that sets the tone for living and co-existing with pain and loss.

I have learned hope is a constant, but constantly transforming to meet one's individual needs. What one hopes for at the time of diagnosis may change along the way. Even through the most difficult times, hope is never absent. Those facing advanced disease are not hopeless. Instead of hoping to be cured, they may hope to avoid pain, to retain their dignity, to resolve old issues and conflicts in their lives and for the chance to tell those they love how they feel. Perhaps they have hope of reuniting with those who have passed on before them. But most of all, people have hope that their lives have had meaning and purpose, that they have left behind an imprint, a memory, something of themselves to benefit their children and others. In this way, hope lightens the load and helps one live fully in the moment.

Healing, I've found, is very different than curing or being cured. Cure implies a successful clinical outcome and the eradication of disease from the body. Healing, on the other hand, is born out of self-discovery, part of an inner process, the recovery of the whole self from the trauma of disease and its pervasive impact on every aspect of our lives. Healing takes place over time. It is a process–and a person can be cured even before they are healed, just as they can be healed without ever being cured.

I have always believed that cancer is a metaphor for the many malignancies we face in life. Whether we are dealing with a tumor, an addiction, or a destructive relationship, we have to battle a plethora of lifelong challenges and losses; however, what matters most is not what such events do to us, but rather, what we do with these events.

A young woman with very advanced cancer once shared her wisdom with me, her words conveyed with unforgettable calm, peace, and faith: "Where I live, we get cloudy winters. With clouds day after day, it's easy to get depressed. So now when I get up in the morning and look out the window, even if it's a cloudy day, I say, thank you God, I've got one more day. I don't see the clouds, because I know the sun is shining above them."

It is with such faith that we cope, hope, and endure.

Selma R. Schimmel is the CEO and founder of Vital Options® International TeleSupport® Cancer Network, a not-for-profit organization based in Southern California. She started the outreach organization in 1983 after her breast cancer diagnosis. Each Sunday, she talks with more than half a million listeners affected by cancer when she hosts The Group Room, a nationally syndicated weekly radio call-in talk show. Her book, *Cancer Talk: Voices of Hope and Endurance from 'The Group Room,' the World's Largest Cancer Support Group* (Broadway Books, 1999), was inspired by these national conversations.

I Want to Hold Your Hand
Jacob Pressman

She lay precisely in the middle of her hospital bed. She looked serene and more lovely than she had in recent years. The bedrails were down. The intravenous needle was gone from above her wrist, and its drip-measuring meter was silent and dark. Someone had valiantly attempted to comb her hair. Her eyes were closed. Her face was relaxed. Her lips were blue.

Her family members, who had kept a faithful vigil by her side for days, had been sent home. I had called them from my study just before they left, to inquire how she was doing. In a voice dampened by tears, her daughter told me that there was no point in coming. She had turned cold and blue, and the nurses had suggested that they go home and rest up for the new ordeal of seeing to it that she was given the proper last rites. Reluctantly they had all left, declining to see her beloved face covered by the sheet. "Don't trouble yourself to come," her daughter said, "Your prayers were not answered."

I knew it was late in the afternoon, and that I faced a taxing evening after a quick dinner. While it was too late for me to recite the Vidui, the final confessional, with her, I was somehow drawn to see her once more. She should not be alone. I decided to go to the hospital.

At her bedside I stood, feeling not grief, but some of the serenity her face and body reflected. I took her wrist and was momentarily shocked. It was ice cold. Instinctively and not fully aware of what I was doing, I began to massage her limp hand, whispering to her all the many memories of shared congregational and family gatherings, even recalling moments I had not brought to mind for years. My hands were rubbing hers, and my breath was in her face, though I acted without conscious thought. The room was darkening as the day waned, but the overhead reading light glowed all the brighter on her face.

Unaccountably, it seemed to me her wrist was getting warm. Her lips took on a bit of rosy color. I stared at her in disbelief and spoke now above a whisper, calling her name, saying we all loved her and needed her. After another long time, or so it seemed, her eyelids began to flutter and finally opened. Her blue eyes looked into mine at first without recognition, but gradually seemed more and more aware of my presence. She actually whispered, "Rabbi, thank you for coming. Excuse me; I am very sleepy."

She closed her eyes again, but this time her chest rose and fell ever so delicately. My right hand never let go of hers, but my left frantically pressed the call button over and over until a nurse came. What happened next is somewhat blurred in my memory, but staff people appeared, there was activity and someone said, "Rabbi, let go! Let go! You are in the way!"

She lived another nine years. We even danced together at a Temple affair. Neither of us ever mentioned that not-quite-final scene to family or friends, even when her daughter said, "Thank God you were there when she came back from the other side." However, when the occasion permitted, we would give each other a knowing wink.

We may live in an age of "miracle" medicine, but the true miracles, of love and warmth and touch and hope and faith, were at work in the world long before we existed and will persist long after we are gone. I pray it may be so.

Rabbi Jacob Pressman, MHL, DHL, DD, is Rabbi Emeritus of Temple Beth Am in Los Angeles and has been a founder of Jewish and educational institutions throughout Southern California, including the University of Judaism, Brandeis-Bardin and The Camp Ramah in Ojai, California, Pressman Academy, and the Beverly Hills Maple Center. He's the author of *Dear Friends: A Prophetic Journey Through Great Events of the 20th Century* (Ktav, 2002), *This Wild and Crazy World as Seen From Beverly Hills* (Jacob Pressman, 2002), and *The Hebrew Alphabet* (Triton, 1988).

Good Deeds

Loving-kindness is greater than laws; and the charities of life are more than all ceremonies.
– *The Talmud*

Sailing Toward Healing
Sherri Mandell

A woman I don't know telephones. She says that she read my book, *The Blessing of a Broken Heart*, and she wants me to know I will be happy again, one day, despite the death of my 13-year-old son, Koby, who was viciously murdered by terrorists, two and half years ago. This woman's brother died 40 years ago in Brazil, and her mother, she claims, is now a happy woman. She says that in my book, I compare my pain to a rock thrown into a pond. After each ripple comes another circle of pain. She wants to reassure me that the circles will stop; there will be an end.

I don't believe her. I ask a physicist about the circles of the pond. He says that the ripples do end, because of the friction of the water; they simply subside. I realize that I need to pick another metaphor, because I am sure that I will always feel the ripples of pain of my son's death. In fact, many people who have lost children told my husband and me that the pain gets worse with the years. I choose not to believe them. But I don't believe the pain will ever totally recede. Perhaps I don't want it to. It is now part of my relationship with Koby. The pain tells me how precious is my love for my son.

I do not and will never have that vaunted "closure" that American popular culture loves to extol. But I am working toward healing. Healing is a journey, not a destination.

Creating a foundation in memory of my son is part of that healing. We established the Koby Mandell Foundation, which runs camps and healing retreats for family members who have lost loved ones to terror. Once during a mothers' healing retreat, we took a group of 15 bereaved women sailing along the coast of Herzliya to Tel Aviv. Before we boarded, I told the women that when our children were murdered, it was like we had been thrown overboard, in danger of drowning. Now we had to find a way to get back onto the ship, claim our sea legs, and discover a new way of moving in the world. Momentarily pleased with the aptness of my metaphor, I boarded the sailboat.

After a few minutes, I felt nauseous and anxious. Soon, I felt sick to my stomach. Immediately I realized that the only way I could handle this trip was to focus on the farthest point, on the horizon, and keep my glance outward. That attitude, that vision embodied how I was living with grief.

The way I heal is by shifting my focus away from what's closest, what I don't have. If I keep thinking of all I have lost, I am unable to get out of bed, attend a wedding, or even relate to the world. If I keep thinking of all I am missing in losing my son, I can drown in a minute. Instead, I think of what I have and where I am heading. Of course, it doesn't always work. I cry for my loss and feel sorry for my family. But because I have turned my vision toward a bigger future, I survive. That bigger view now includes sharing my experience of pain, grief, and healing–giving others the support I feel in my own community.

The physicist I spoke to explained something else to me–when you throw a rock into the water, the level of the water rises–that is what creates the ripples. In a strange way, my son's death has also caused me to rise from my past experience. My life has been exalted and hallowed by the loss of my son, motivating me to lead a richer, more meaningful existence. Koby has become my compass. His absence now orients me in the world, guiding me to do more, to make my life more significant, so that his death counts, so that it means something, so that it matters.

Healing is a horizon that stays in the distance, one I keep sailing toward.

Seth and Sherri Mandell moved to Israel from America in 1996 because they loved Israel and wanted Judaism to occupy a central place in the life of their family. Their lives were devastated in 2001, when their 13-year-old son, Koby, was murdered. Koby went hiking with his friend, Yosef Ish Ran, in a canyon near the Mandell's home. There, in a cave, Arab terrorists stoned the two boys to death. The Mandells, parents to three other younger children, knew that in order to go on, they needed to transform the cruelty of Koby's death into acts of kindness and hope. They created the Koby Mandell Foundation (www.kobymandell.org), which provides healing programs for families who have lost a mother, father, sister, or brother through terrorism. Seth, a rabbi, and Sherri, an author and journalist, believe that the Jewish response to suffering is to live a fuller and more engaged life. Sherri is the director of the Foundation's Women's Healing Retreat for Bereaved Mothers and Widows, and the author of *The Blessing of a Broken Heart* (Toby Press, 2003).

Eclair Epiphany
Jackie Waldman

There are unexpected moments in our lives, good and bad, that can change us forever. July 12, 1991, the day I was diagnosed with multiple sclerosis, was my bad moment.

At the time I had no idea what MS was; I thought it was what "Jerry's kids" have and was relieved to discover I was wrong. But, when I learned about MS–an autoimmune disease with no cure–I was terrified. I remember crying and hugging my husband, Steve, and telling him how sorry I was. He told me we would get through this together. I also remember telling our children, Melissa, Todd, and Michael, that MS is not hereditary, I wouldn't die from the disease, and nothing in our lives would change. But everything changed, because I changed.

I spent the next five years feeling sorry for myself, mourning the loss of my old life, wondering why me, and withdrawing from my family and friends. One night at dinner, I fell asleep sitting at the table. When I woke up I was holding a half-eaten chocolate éclair, and custard was smeared across my face. Suddenly I saw what I had become. I thought to myself, "If I'm like this now, what will I be like in a year, five years? I have got to make some changes, but I don't even know where to begin. I've felt sorry for myself for so long."

I've come to understand that my éclair experience was a spiritual surrender. At that moment I was ready to let go of the negative feelings I had lived with since being diagnosed—the sadness, anger, and fear. When we're ready to accept our limitations and see new possibilities, something will come along to move us forward on this new path. For me, it was seeing the film *Schindler's List*. After watching the Oskar Schindler character save over 1,000 lives and still wish he could save one more, after seeing the courage of the people who suffered so terribly under Nazi rule, I realized what I had done wrong for so many years. I had thought survival was completely tied to my old life, to the narrow question of whether my legs and body could work like they used to. Finally, I realized true survival is survival of our spirit, no matter what.

I visited the Dallas Holocaust Memorial Center, trained to become a docent, and began speaking with middle school and high school students just once a week. As I spoke with them about the Holocaust, about the power of individual acts of kindness, about the responsibility each of us has to the greater good, I felt the truth of my words.

Sometimes the experiences we have are so terrible, so painful, that we wonder how we will ever go on. It takes great courage to release the past, to move forward in a powerful way and make a difference for others. When we choose to find the courage to give, especially when we are suffering, something miraculous happens—we rediscover the sweetness of life.

My life is not just OK—it's better—because I have MS.

Jackie Waldman's first book, The Courage to Give (MJF Books, 2000), shares 30 stories of people who have had something happen to them physically and/or emotionally, yet when they started helping others, their lives changed miraculously. A subsequent appearance on Oprah drew attention to Jackie's mission of promoting random acts of kindness. Within 36 hours of the show's airing, more than 7,500 people signed up to volunteer with a charity they found using the website Jackie suggested during the show –volunteermatch.org. Since then, Jackie has compiled four more books of inspiring stories: *Teens with the Courage to Give; America, September 11: The Courage to Give; Teachers with the Courage to Give* and her new book, *People with MS with the Courage to Give*. Visit www.couragetogive.com.

For Those Beloved Who Survive Me
Harold M. Schulweis

Mourn me not with tears, ashes, or sackcloth.
Nor dwell in darkness, sadness, or remorse.
Remember that I love you, and wish for you a life of song.
My immortality, if there be such for me, is not in tears,
blame or self-recrimination.
But in the joy you give to others, in raising the fallen
and loosening the fetters of the bound.
In your loyalty to God's special children – the widow, the orphan,
the poor, the stranger in your gates, the weak – I take pride.

The fringes of the tallit placed on my body are torn, for the dead
cannot praise You, O Lord.
The dead have no mitzvot.
But your tallit is whole and you are alive
and alive you are called to mitzvot.
You can choose, you can act, you can transform the world.

My immortality is bound up with God's eternity, with God's
justice, truth and righteousness.
And that eternity is strengthened by your loyalty and your love.
Honor me with laughter and with goodness.
With these, the better part of me lives on beyond the grave.

Harold M. Schulweis is arguably the best-known pulpit rabbi in America. Combining a Talmudic education with graduate studies in modern philosophical and theological thought, he received advanced degrees at New York University, the Jewish Theological Seminary, and the Pacific School of Religion in Berkeley, California, from which he received his Th.D. He has authored many books, including *For Those Who Can't Believe* (Harper Collins, 1994), *In God's Mirror* (Ktav, 1990) and the classic *Evil and the Morality of God* (HUC Press, 1983). Rabbi Schulweis has lectured in philosophy and theology at CCNY, the University of Judaism, and Hebrew Union College. He is the founding chairman of the Jewish Foundation for the Righteous, which identifies and offers grants to non-Jews who risked their lives to save Jews threatened by the agents of Nazi savagery. Rabbi Schulweis is Senior Rabbi of Congregation Valley Beth Shalom in Encino, California.

Going Home, Going Home
Kirk Douglas

This essay was excerpted from Mr. Douglas' most recent book,
My Stroke of Luck (Perennial, 2003), with the permission of the author

When I returned from my travels, I entered my room and stretched out on the bed, my little safety net during the early days after my stroke. This is where it all happened. There was the chair that I sat in when I felt the thin line trace across my cheek. This is the room where I did so many oral aerobics. It was here that I devised an Operator's Manual, which enabled me to go out into the world again.

As I lay on my bed, Danny and Foxy jumped up and started licking at me. They were glad to see me. I was happy. My stroke had led me on a great adventure and changed me into a different person—a person whom I like.

Happiness is a temporary state. Waves of depression continue to ebb and flow, a relentless tide, no matter how hard I strive to subdue them. I have learned to live with uncertainty, to know that in life, there are no guarantees. I have learned that no matter how much you believe your house to be a safe haven, a fortress against the dangers of living, the hand of fate can pass through to touch you lightly on the shoulder, to smite you and your loved ones, to draw, with a sharp pointed line, on your cheek, from your temple to your chin.

When you feel too weak to carry your burden, look to the actions of other human beings for inspiration. Embedded in my mind is the Seattle Special Olympics of a few years ago. A story was told to me about nine contestants, all physically or mentally disabled, assembled at the starting line for the hundred-yard dash.

At the gun, they all started out, not exactly in a dash, but with a relish for running the race to the finish and winning. All, that is, except one little boy, who stumbled on the asphalt, tumbled over a couple of times, and began to cry.

The other eight heard the boy cry. They slowed down and looked back. Then they all turned around and went back…every one of them.

One girl with Down's syndrome bent down and kissed him and said, "This will make it better." Then all nine linked arms and walked together to the finish line. Everyone in the stadium stood, and the cheering went on for several minutes. People who were there are still telling the story.

Why? Because deep down we know that what matters in this life is more than winning for ourselves. What matters in this life is helping others win, even if it means slowing down and changing our course. We all want happiness. Life teaches us that we achieve happiness when we seek the happiness and well-being of others.

I started writing this book to try and help people understand a stroke, and find a way to deal with it and function in life. I wanted to construct an Operator's Manual that would be a guide for recovering from a stroke. My stroke taught me so much, and for all that it stole, it gave me even more. In the process of healing, my life has changed for the better. Now I want to share what I have learned.

But in looking over my Operator's Manual, I had an epiphany. Dealing with a stroke, dealing with any ailment or misfortune, is no different from the way we all should live our lives.

My Operator's Manual

1. When things go bad, always remember it could be worse.
2. Never, never give up. Keep working on your speech and on your life.
3. Never lose your sense of humor. Laugh at yourself, laugh with others.
4. Stem depression by thinking of, reaching out to, and helping others. Strive to be a Little Hero.
5. Do unto others as you would have them do unto you.
6. Pray. Not for God to cure you, but to help you help yourself.

Helen Keller, blind and deaf from birth, said, "When we do the best we can, we never know what miracle is wrought in our life, or the life of another."

We all have a handicap—big or small. But we must overcome our hardships to become better people. We must try, we must try.

Kirk Douglas forged a memorable career playing restless, impassioned characters (*Champion, Lust for Life, Spartacus*) in a body of work that has spanned six decades and earned him three Academy Award nominations as Best Actor. Douglas became a bestselling author with the publication of *The Ragman's Son*, an unflinching memoir of his childhood as the son of extremely poor Russian-Jewish immigrants. His most recent book, excerpted here, is an account of his physical and spiritual recovery from a debilitating stroke.

Art: Words, Images, & Music

As long as the soul animates man, and longs for light and thirsts for beauty,
man needs the fountain of poetry.
– *Chaim Nachman Bialik*

Speaking from Pain:
Poetry as Reverse Mi Sheberach
William Cutter

Faced with illness, many of us seek a bit of light in prayer or poetry, or at the very least, we manage to reach out in the dark. We are finite, and God is infinite; when our limitations cause us suffering, we seek the infinite to ameliorate our finitude. Prayer aptly expresses this act of reaching out, but it's poetry that has spoken most directly to my own struggles and painful experiences, sparking meaningful introspection.

I turn to familiar poems—certainly those in English, as well as poetry from across the canon of Western culture, but my favorite poems come from the literary geniuses of our Hebrew language. Written in the historical tongue that has so richly occupied the Jewish spirit, it's poetry that contains spiritual insights cast in a Jewish cultural frame. These poems have become private supplements to both my *Mi Sheberach* (prayers for the healing and recovery of the sick) and my highly personal, less communal prayers of the heart. They give me a more direct relationship with illness and the struggles of the human spirit.

I value poems that heighten the intimacy we feel when we are in a room with others; I learn from poems that acknowledge a patient's helplessness, especially if that helplessness succeeds a life that has been distinguished by vigor and accomplishment. I'm struck by poems that address the religious doubt that can demoralize the caregiver. Many poems convey the relentless length of illness; others renew and enhance our awareness of death's presence, and the presence, too, of all those who hover and linger in our midst even after death.

Some of the poems and stories I love most draw trenchantly on a phrase or idea from Jewish tradition. When the poet Abba Kovner lay in his cancer ward, he recalled his helplessness through the traditional words of the Hazzan at Yom Kippur: "Behold I am humble of deed," he offered, somewhat sarcastically. The Russian-born writer, "Zelda," who emigrated to Israel and published her poetry in Hebrew, compares the nearly tragic moan of a loved one to a voice first heard in the Book of Amos, muffled as if coming from the bottom of the ocean floor. Modern Israeli poet Malka Shaked asserts her religious skepticism when she writes that resurrection was an idea long buried. She dismissively compares practicing the recitation of the *Shema* to tuning her violin. The well-loved Israeli poet, Yehuda Amichai, compares the fib a boy tells his parents—"I went to a different synagogue"–to the lies parents tell in order to reassure children—dead parents "have gone to another life."

In the narratives of the Jewish tradition, we find poetic thoughts that elevate our spirit. *El-na, refa-na lah*, ("Heal Her, Please"–Moses' prayer for his sick sister, Miriam), is about as lyrical an expression of hope as one may find in any language.

In our own time, the link between human need and poetic expression is explained matter-of-factly by Yehuda Amichai: "I learned to speak from my pain."

We live between harshness and hope. We seek words to express our yearnings, which are as infinite as the evening shadows (another Amichai image). Our hope and our longings may be infinite, yet we seek finite solutions.

Four centuries ago, John Donne observed that we are the profane authors and the seed of the serpent, while God is the Dove that flies. Our poets reflect our reach up from the dust toward the heavens. They depict the way we wrestle with our very finite and concrete humanity. In another poem, Amichai connects this struggle to the ladder Father Jacob still carries to foster humanity's upward progress:

> He will climb up that ladder if ever he dies,
> right out of this world and into the skies,
> until the world vanishes into this air
> For all that we know he is still climbing there.
> ~tr. by Chana Bloch and Chana Kronfeld

The *Nishmat* prayer of the morning service insists that we lack language to express the utter majesty of God and God's world. And so we seek metaphors. With poetic language and imagery, we assert our physicality and stretch toward hope. We learn to speak from our pain.

William Cutter teaches at Hebrew Union College-Jewish Institute of Religion, where he is Professor of Hebrew Literature and Education, and Steinberg Professor of Human Relations. He is Director of the Kalsman Institute on Judaism and Health, a center for discourse about health, spirituality, and public policy. He is particularly interested in the conjunction of narrative, poetry, and healing.

A Dream for Bezalel
Rodger Kamenetz

Rose gold in the east, chalk blue to the south
when the walls of night come down
and the moon puts out its light.

Who sustained me when arrows flew
from ten directions in a dream:
North and South, up and down,
good and evil, East and West,
Long Gone and Long to Come.

Ten arrows pointed at the walls
and vessels of my heart.
I told the arrow heads, Dig in.
But my heart would not yield.

The arrows circled into a shield
rose gold, Adam's translucent nail.
Rose gold in the east, blue black in the west
when the sun rose, my heart was lit and healed.

Rose gold in the east, mouths of light
through live oak leaves. The E of East
speeds down sleek hills.
Birds attack the first
burnt notes of song.
This is the season of Av.

Two days past cries of mourning
dust on my forehead, scraps of sack in my hair
the temple ruins reassemble themselves.
The doors meet their jambs, the windows open on air,
an old widow's cry marries hoarse chants
of a creaking bed. Dust springs to flesh,
fingers stretch to search the light.
The mourning dove descends and cries.
False light departs, fresh light stirs
in every vowel and cell.

August, I get up with dawn.
I go to the gold cabinet.
I smile in the mirror.
This is a day given to me.
Already small branches
sprout tufts of light.
Dew rides wiry spindles
where grass bends and bows.
The slick street carries
a squeal and clatter,
the circulation begins:

Rose gold in the east, molten fire below
the sky lifts its pastel dome.
Already the sun has done its work...
Shall I delay?

for R. Duvid Blank

Poet, essayist, teacher, and religious thinker, Rodger Kamenetz has been called by critics "one of the most formidable of Jewish voices of American poetry." He is the author of eight books, among them the much-loved *The Jew in the Lotus* (Harper 1995), an account of a unique Buddhist-Jewish dialogue in Dharamsala between the Dalai Lama and a delegation of American Jews (the author among them). *Stalking Elijah* (Harper 1997), his exploration of contemporary Jewish mysticism, won the National Jewish Book Award. His books of poetry include *Stuck, The Missing Jew: New and Selected Poems* and most recently, *The Lowercase Jew* (Northwestern University Press (2003). Kamenetz teaches in the MFA Program at Louisiana State University.

Shirei Shalom (Songs of Peace)
Theodore Bikel

It was the Yom Kippur War.

The year was 1973, and Israel was in its hour of isolation. If I didn't do what I could, as an artist and as an American Jew, to lend whatever prestige and talent I had to the struggle in person, then all of the speeches I had given and all the rallies I had attended over the years in support of Israel would not count for much. I contacted the Israelis, announcing my readiness to help. I flew with a planeload of young men returning to join their army units. Since the outbreak of war, regular El Al flights had been suspended. All available planes had been put to such use as the government and the military required.

Tel Aviv had a different face when I arrived; there were no tourists, and the town, one of the liveliest I had ever known, was dead. In the Tel Aviv Hilton where I had been assigned a room, the only other civilians were war correspondents from all over the world. But the hotel was teeming with men and women in uniform, doing liaison chores and conducting briefings.

I had not come as a journalist or as an observer or as a fighter. I did want to go to the trenches and so I had brought the only weapon I have–or care to have–my guitar. The army assigned me a car and driver, as well as a liaison officer. First I was taken to hospitals where the wounded had been brought from the battlefields. Arriving as I had from peaceful America, what I saw was shocking to the senses, but I had come to help. I played and sang in large and small hospital rooms, initially for men who were lightly wounded and could laugh and clap, but also for the severely wounded who could barely acknowledge they were able to hear.

The nursing staff encouraged me to persevere; music seemed to have a therapeutic effect, even on these patients. One of the most gratifying moments occurred in a hospital wing where severely shell-shocked soldiers were being treated. There was one man who had been in a catatonic state ever since they had brought him in. His tank had been blown up by a direct hit; miraculously, he survived, but the doctors doubted he could ever come out of his severe mental trauma. Fed through tubes, he had been in this one position for several days; he reacted to nothing. I played in his room for a long while and suddenly there was a small foot movement; he was tapping to the beat of the music. The nurses started to cry. They hugged him and me, and I too had tears in my eyes. The song I sang most often then was Jacques Brel's "If We Only Have Love." I sang it in Hebrew and in English.

A few years later, when the peace process that was sparked by Anwar Sadat's famous trip to Jerusalem culminated with the Washington signing of a treaty between Israel and Egypt, I was there. Invited to attend a reception for the very gracious Madame Jihan Sadat and asked to perform, I decided to sing the Brel song, again in English and in Hebrew, before the dignitaries: Arabs, Jews, and many others. I explained that I had sung that same song at a time and in a place where bombs were exploding all around us and shrapnel was flying; I would sing it again on this night.

My recalling these events raised a few eyebrows: Madame Sadat asked why I chose to recall strife and bloodshed at a time of joy. I assured her that in my view it was all a part of the healing process. If you are not willing to remember the bitter times, then you cannot fully savor the sweet taste of peace.

In his own words, Theodore Bikel is not a "specialist but a general practitioner in the world of the arts." Many people associate him with his folk music albums or his acclaimed stage performances as Tevye, in *Fiddler on the Roof*, a role he has played over 2,000 times. Yet Bikel has also touched people all over the world as an opera performer, theater and film actor, lecturer, author, raconteur, activist, and concerned human being.

The Passage of Time

Would that life were like the shadow cast by a wall or a tree,
but it is like the shadow of a bird in flight.
– *The Talmud*

Loss/Lost in Translation
Diane Arieff

I stood at the checkout counter at Whole Foods, observing the teenaged cashier who was ringing me up. Her forearms were tattooed from wrist to elbow, heavy with ink like pages from a comic book. She wore rings on her thumbs and was pierced in all the standard places. The low-slung jeans she wore exposed a stomach still soft with baby fat. I was only in my late thirties, but I might as well have been observing her from an alternate universe, light years away. When her cell phone went off, she fished it out of her back pocket and held it to her mouth, still scanning my groceries and sliding them down the conveyor belt while she talked, not missing a beat. Her side of the conversation went like this:

"What do you want?"
(pause)
"Mom, what do you WANT?"
(pause)
"I told you not to call me at work."
(eye rolling)
"I don't care. Don't call me at work."
(pause)
"Mom, just stop bugging me, ok? I'm fine."
(pause)
"I'm not sure when I'll be home."
(eye rolling)
"Because you bug me. Omygod, just leave me alone."
(loud sigh)
"Look, I have to go. I have to GO. Don't call me!"

It was painful enough to make me wince. My own mother had died just the year before. There were still times I found myself reaching for the phone to call her. Near the end, in one of those suspended hours of time we spent alone together, she squeezed my hand and said, almost sternly, "We don't have any unfinished business. I know how much you love me."

Her death was still fresh. It had left me feeling skinless and unprotected. One afternoon, when I came across the word "motherless" in a book, I was startled, as if someone had shouted my name.

In one of her published letters, Edna St. Vincent Millay wrote, "Where you used to be, there is a hole in the world." Yes, I thought. Exactly. I carried her lines around with me for months.

Grief, I came to understand, is like a fierce initiation rite for the heart. Standing there at the market, I watched the GothPunk girl click off her cell phone and shake her head in irritation. It's possible her mother was uniquely monstrous, but somehow, I doubted it.

She handed me my receipt, uninterested in eye contact. Something welled up inside of me and I stayed where I was, hesitant but determined to step outside the bounds of our transaction.

"Look," I said softly as I tucked my wallet into my purse. My voice shook. "Don't be too hard on your mother if you can help it. She won't be around forever." A look of surprise flickered across her face, probably because of the audacity of such a thing, this woman she didn't even know, this loopy *customer*. She shrugged, annoyed with me but playing it cool, and turned back toward the register.

In the parking lot, as I loaded the grocery bags into my trunk, I wondered if I should have held my tongue. I meant to give her some simple but important thing, a small existential "heads up." But really, why should this prickly teenaged girl with a tongue stud have listened to me? I was speaking a language she had no use for yet. From where I stood, on my side of the divide, the message I was sending seemed painfully clear, but it was lost in translation.

Maybe that was how it should be. In a perfect world of answered prayers, no children would ever be on intimate terms with despair. All teenagers would regard mortality and death as distant abstractions, like global warming or the stock exchange.

She should have been kinder to her mother, true. But not for the reasons I gave her. Those she would come to later, in her own time, with her own losses, the way Edna and I had in ours.

The editor of this book, Diane Arieff, began her career as a freelance writer and editor in high school, when she started sending off bad poetry to literary journals and humor essays to newspapers. (The latter sometimes got published.) Formerly an arts editor at the *Jewish Journal of Los Angeles*, Arieff's work has appeared in many publications, including the *Los Angeles Times*, the *Milwaukee Journal*, the *Daily News*, and the *Chicago Sun-Times*.

The Circle of Life
Susan Whitmore

After eleven long hours of pain, there she was–chestnut brown hair, vivid blue eyes, cute pug nose, round face and full lips. She was so beautiful. It was instant love. I knew in that moment that my life would never be the same.

The circle of life had begun.

The year was 1970, and her name was Erika. She was my only child. I was a happy, contented mother. Erika was everything to me–my meaning and purpose in life. We traveled through our lives together, never taking our gift of love for granted.

Thirty years had flown by, and Erika had grown into a beautiful and caring woman. As we busily prepared for her wedding, we were bubbling with excitement. I was so proud of who she was. But it was not to be. Sometimes life simply has its own plans. So it was in our case. As we listened in utter disbelief, we heard the diagnosis: Erika had a rare form of cancer.

Our circle of life had been assaulted.

If prayers could save a person's life, then Erika would have lived forever. We learned that not all prayers are answered in just the way they are asked. In May 2002, as we surrounded and enfolded Erika with our bodies and encouraged her with our love, I once again gazed into her beautiful blue eyes, as this time she took her last breath. I could not believe what my eyes and broken heart told me were true.

After eleven long months of pain, there she was–chestnut brown hair, vivid blue eyes, cute pug nose, round face, and full lips. She would forever remain as beautiful. I knew in that moment that my life would never be the same again.

The circle of life had been broken.

I will forever be Erika's mother. Nothing changes that. As the days move forward and I continue my journey of life without Erika, I miss everything about her: her laugh, smile, smell, beauty, creativity, her loving and giving ways, her giggle, advice, disagreements, long phone calls, our meals together, shopping, vacations, being called "mom," and the way she made me feel about myself as a person, mother, and friend.

No one can tell another how to grieve. Grieving the loss of a child does not come with a "how to" manual. Our individual ways of grieving are as different as our genes, and grief is not a linear process. At first, I'd wished myself dead; I couldn't eat or sleep. Everything hurt—even the radiant color of a flower. I had lost all meaning and purpose in life. I was learning to accept that this was not something I would ever just "get over." Just yesterday in fact, I found myself curled up in a ball, sobbing uncontrollably over the pain, and yet, today is okay. As the minutes, hours, days, and weeks evolve, life begins to feel worth living again. I realize finally that the only wrong way to grieve is not to grieve at all.

Just as the scars on a precious antique are markers of the life it has led, so too do my scars of loss mark out my grief. What keeps me going day after day is the undying love and support of those who promised to stick by me without placing a time limit on my sadness. The pain may not abate, not after one year, or five, or ten. To others, such periods might seem sufficient for healing and closure, but for grieving parents, a year is a mere blink of an eye.

Hope is the only true magic word for me, for with hope I can endure the heart-wrenching reality of Erika's absence; hope that it will get easier with hard work and time; hope that I will go on to live a meaningful life, as others have done; and hope that my indescribable loss will lead to help for others traveling this unwanted path of grief.

In that spirit of hope, we have come full circle.

Susan Whitmore is Founder and President of The Erika Whitmore Godwin Foundation and of Grief Haven, which provides hope and critical support to parents and families who have lost a child. She is also the producer of the documentary *Portraits of Grief; Badges of Courage*. Visit www.griefHaven.org.

The Watch
Elisa Albert

My brother David and I shared a wicked, sick sense of humor. And similarly shaped feet. That's about it. He was a full nine years older than I, which granted us relatively little childhood bonding time. He was off to college before I hit puberty, which was fine with me. Truth be told: he was what I, in my junior-high parlance, deemed a "dork." My diagnosis was based not only on his affinity for information about the space program, or his encyclopedic knowledge of *Star Trek*–there was also his watch, an iconically futuristic contraption, something George Orwell or an animator for *The Jetsons* might have conjured up: bulky and black with almost a full keyboard and little screen. The only thing it couldn't do was your taxes. He delighted in taking it off to demonstrate its many capabilities.

David frustrated me. Our age difference, the watch, his fondness for science fiction, our similar stubbornness, and the fact that a brain tumor killed him at 29 meant that we never truly got to be friends. I loathe the judgmental, shallow adolescent I was, but of course, it's too late now. David's gone, and as I come ever closer to understanding, he's never coming back. I dearly hope he knew how much I love(d) him. We exchanged many such sentiments in the months before he died, but I am filled with fear that the paradigm of bratty little sister vs. science nerd big brother is, in the end, the sum of the relationship that this lifetime afforded us.

He has been dead for (can it be?) almost six years, and I have his watch now, tucked away at the bottom of my jewelry box. I take it out every few days or weeks. For the first few years after his death, the watch maintained its date and time with characteristic NASA-like precision, unfailingly greeting me with correct information. Tuesday, March 10, 1999, 12:19 am. I felt I could raise and set the sun to David's watch, a huge relief, really: it was the lone continuity I could link to him. David did not exist, but anytime I wanted, I could unearth his quaintly dorky digital watch and orient myself exactly with the stars, within the universe.

Time marched on, and somehow, clutching his still-accurate watch, that was quite all right, almost as though he himself, from beyond the grave, had sanctioned such a thing.

It's okay, the watch told me, flashing a date and time in the irrevocably AD (after David) era, *live your life*, Tisha (his nickname for me, based on my own earliest attempts to pronounce my name).

When I press the button that switches the setting, the name "Manuel" flashes on the screen, alongside a phone number. Manuel was David's hospice nurse, a sweet, five-foot tall Andean man with a shiny black ponytail and stunningly kind bedside manner. The recollection of David, towards the very end of his short life, his eyes drooping and jaw slackened by the life ebbing out of him, asking lovely Manuel for his phone number and then painstakingly entering it via the tiny buttons on his dorky digital watch, is one of the only things that can bring forth fresh tears in me.

Each time I take out the watch, I brace myself for a dead or even slower battery, terrified of what this will mean, of how it will feel to see the face blank. The battery surely won't last forever. In recent days it has begun, finally, to slow down.

"Why don't you just get the battery replaced before it dies?" my mom gently suggested not long ago.

"No," I said. "I don't want to do that." But I couldn't quite articulate why. It has something to do with letting go, though. I know that much. When the watch dies, it will be appropriate and final and peaceful. I hope it helps me feel ready to say goodbye.

Elisa Albert is an MFA candidate in the fiction-writing program at Columbia University. Her work has appeared in *Pindeldyboz*, *Response, The Jewish Journal of Los Angeles* and in *Body Outlaws: Rewriting the Rules of Body Image and Identity* (Seal Press, 2004).

Seven Keys to Healing

Janet Sternburg

I wish I could tell my parents that something in me has changed. I had said there's only a chaotic and impersonal force in the universe. But when I found myself crying "What did I do wrong?" I joined an ancient line of human beings calling out for answers.

from *Phantom Limb: A Memoir*

The first key: Awareness. In a crisis, we're so often consumed by the immediate needs of the situation that we forget our physical bodies. STOP. LOOK. Check your sense of balance. Awareness can keep you from falling.

The second key: Remembering. Conventional wisdom says we move on, don't dwell. While that may be fine in some situations, I think there's a price to be paid. Deep healing begins with a willingness to remain open, to live with pain. Is remembering worth it when it's painful? Yes? Look at what else it brings: sweetness, poignancy, savoring. We need to use memory as a friend.

The third key: Revising. Healing also arises from the willingness to have second thoughts, not to obsess, nor even necessarily to analyze, but to remain open to asking yourself, "Was that really the way it was?"

The fourth key: Evolving, by which I mean working toward a world-view. For some, that dimension is provided by organized religion; others create their individual perspective. The essential idea is to see your own existence as part of something larger than yourself. In the search for consolation, the search itself is all-important.

The fifth key: Submitting. A religious friend said to me, "This is God's football. You're writing about what concerns everyone: what is life going to throw you?" In my memoir, I write about how I tried to rescue my parents from their illnesses. Instead, I found out how much is uncertain, how much cannot be fixed. Understanding the limits of our will, that often we are powerless, is part of the healing process.

The sixth key: Passing on your story, not as an example, but as a way to let others know what you have reaped. You can be a source from which people draw strength.

The seventh key: Understanding the nature of healing, that it's never over and done with. Don't look at healing as a process with a recognizable end, as though you were to remove a Band-Aid, and find that you're as good as new. We're never as good as new. We wouldn't want to be. Recognize that you're not only healing after a specific crisis or a specific wound. You're carrying with you all the wounds and all the healing that you've already experienced. You're carrying with you life itself.

Janet Sternburg is the author of the memoir *Phantom Limb* (Univ. of Nebraska Press, 2002) and the critically praised two-volume collection *The Writer on Her Work* (W.W. Norton, 2000). She teaches writing at the California Institute of the Arts and is also an accomplished photographer. Portfolios of her work can be seen in the Spring 2002 issues of *Aperture* and *Art Forum*. www.janetsternburg.com.

The Wisdom of Surrender

There is no worship, no music, no love, if we take for granted the blessings or defeats of living.
– *Rabbi Abraham Joshua Heschel*

Mugging

Lisa Wolfe

Women of different cultures excel at different things: chewing whale hide, skinning frogs, carrying firewood on top of their heads. As a young professional in New York during the '80's, what I shone at was being a control freak.

Maybe this wasn't attractive, but it seemed essential. I was raised by my frustrated mother and feminist professors to be an empowered woman, and I couldn't figure how else to do this but by micromanaging everything from my career to the shape of my abs.

Eventually I got married and pregnant—and shocked. I had planned to take charge of my pregnancy, but it took charge of me. As my body assumed the shape of a manatee, my brain transformed into the infant rice cereal I'd soon be making, and my ambition dwindled down to wanting to lie on the sofa all day, I couldn't help feeling I had let myself—and womanhood—down.

One afternoon, nearly eight months along, I left work early to vegetate at home. I had my key in the door when I heard a voice behind me ask, "Excuse me, do you know Tony Roberts?"

When I turned I saw a huge man coming at me, his hands lunging for my neck. He pushed me into the house and onto the floor, beating me as I shouted for help. "I'm pregnant!" I cried, as if anyone with eyesight could not have noticed. He grabbed my wrist, snapped it broken, and punched me in the head. As the room spun all I could think was, "I can't believe this is how we're going to die!"

The man blindfolded me, tied my hands behind my back, and said, "Take me to the jewelry, and I mean the good stuff. You show me junk and there will be trouble."

I led the way upstairs, realizing I was either going to fall apart or get very strong. Since there was a baby in my belly, the former was just not an option. "Left to the master bedroom," I said at the top of the stairs. "I'll tell you where everything is. Take it. I don't care. All I care about is that you don't hurt my baby."

The man kicked me onto the floor, where I spent the next hour directing him to everything of value in our home and talking incessantly about the baby. "He's a boy," I said. "The first grandchild on both sides of the family. We're naming him Nico."

The man gradually stopped kicking and punching. "I'm not even going to call the police," I said.
"You're not?"
"I don't care about the police. I told you. I only care about my baby."

"I'm not going to hurt your baby!" the guy blurted. "I didn't come here to hurt your baby! I came here because some of us weren't born with silver spoons in our mouths!"

That's when I knew we'd be okay. I shifted my focus from the man to my son, trying to calm him with the deep breathing exercises I'd been learning in prenatal class.

The man took my ATM card and asked for my PIN number. I told him. He said he was going to get cash and if the number was phony there'd be trouble. "By the way," he added, "good luck with your baby."

I pushed the blindfold off with my knee, ran out the house, and hailed a taxi to the police station. As the police questioned me, they marveled at how I handled the situation, saying that by humanizing the baby and myself I probably avoided further injury. "How did you know what to do?" they kept asking.

I just did. The force I'd been cursing for months for making me so fat and stupid and lazy gave me instructions and I simply followed. I have had a harder time knowing which salad dressing to chose from the two hundred on the grocery shelf than knowing what to do that wretched day.

Joy is a strange thing to have felt as the police whizzed me to the hospital, head throbbing, belly distended to the sky. But joy is unmistakably what it was. The mugger left me something more valuable than anything he stole: the realization that maybe losing control of certain things doesn't diminish your power, but enables you to tap whole new sources of it.

Lisa Wolfe, a former associate producer at *60 Minutes*, has written for *Elle*, *Vogue*, *The New York Times Magazine*, and *O, The Oprah Magazine*. She is currently working on a novel.

Learning to Trust

Amy Eilberg

Ten years ago, I was leaving Philadelphia, the place where I grew up and where most of my loved ones lived, and heading for faraway, alien California, taking only my daughter and my husband–a partner in a marriage that I intuitively knew would soon be ending. I was very frightened.

I had wonderful people supporting me–therapists, friends, all assuring me that I could handle whatever would happen. Yet I was still haunted by fear.

Just before the day of the move, I attended my last session of a support group I had been part of for two very special years. I said my farewells and left, yet one woman followed me out into the parking lot. She was a person I didn't feel particularly close to; but for this group, I doubt our paths would ever have crossed. Suddenly, after the usual words of farewell, she said, with complete certainty, "There's someone waiting for you in California." I was stunned. Something in her tone had changed; I felt I was hearing the voice of God. The words stayed with me through what, in fact, turned out to be a very difficult move. For months I'd find myself scanning a room, wondering, "So, who is it that is waiting for me, and why?" In the end, she was right. Her words of trust sustained me until the blessings of that time of my life became clear.

In fearful, uncertain, and despairing times, the hardest thing of all can be finding a sense of trust. Contemporary culture trains us so relentlessly to believe in the material–only that which we can see, measure, and prove. It's hard to cultivate that part of ourselves that believes in the unseen, especially when our life experience has conditioned us to expect a dark uncertain future. When we're in pain and pessimistic, on what can we base a sense of trust?

Our sacred texts–particularly the Siddur we hold in our hands every day–can be the best textbooks for this lesson, if we learn to accept the teaching. To do so, we must move beyond a simplistic understanding of trust. Trusting life does not mean we'll never again know pain. If we're animated by that expectation, we will feel disappointed–even betrayed–again and again.

But we can learn to trust in a more nuanced way that moves us closer to the healing we need. We can learn to trust in the impermanence and changeability of things. It reminds us that even the most intractable pain, the most apparently hopeless situation, will change, as will all experience. It opens us to the possibility that the next day, the next moment, may bring something we could not have anticipated. We can learn to trust in the basic benevolence of life–that the power of healing is great, that the world is full of many loving people, that help is available. And we can learn that there are resources to which we can turn–in those around us, in our own inner capacities, and in whatever we may call God.

A more trusting and nuanced perspective on life rarely cures illness; it may not change the external facts of a situation, but it can transform our experience of it. Trust may make an overwhelming situation manageable, intractable pain bearable, and despair seem temporary, soon to be followed by a new experience.

Another California story. I had been living there for five years. The marriage ended, but for blessing. I had been through a very dark time, but came through, knowing I hadn't merely survived, but had gained whole new vistas in my spiritual life. Life was beautiful. I went for a walk in the hills near my home with a close friend who was going through a terribly painful divorce. She ached for certainty, longing to know how the story would end, yearning to regain the security of knowing with whom she would build a life.

As we walked, we noticed the curves in the path ahead. We realized one can never know what lies beyond the next curve in the road. In comfortable times, we rely on the illusion of pre-dictability. But the truth is, we never know. We must always live in trust that we will be cared for, no matter what.

The ability to trust life may be the most critical skill we master. In my efforts to learn it, I've spent hours contemplating a few favorite Biblical verses (all found in the Siddur): "Blessed is the person who trusts in God, whose Help is in God" (Jeremiah 17:7); "God is my Light and my Help; whom shall I fear?" (Psalms 27:1); "God is my Help; I will trust, I will not fear" (Isaiah 12:2).

Perhaps fully integrating just one image into our lives is enough. It's the final couplet of *Adon Olam: Beyado afkid ruhi be'eit ishan ve'a'ira*, "In Your hand, I place my soul, O God, when I wake and when I sleep." If we cultivate moments of understanding that our souls will be held in loving protection in good times and bad, then we will be on our way to healing.

The first woman ordained by the Jewish Theological Seminary as a Conservative rabbi, Amy Eilberg is a national leader in the Jewish healing movement. She is Co-Director of the Morei Derekh Program for Training in Jewish Spiritual Direction and offers spiritual direction training in private practice.

Of Blessings and Curses

Joel ben Izzy

Of all the tales I've told, this one finds its way back to me more than any other. I am always gratified when I hear it, for I know that it has traveled far, like a salmon swimming upriver to spawn. Usually, by the time it arrives, all that remains is a phrase: "What seems like a curse...."

Sometimes, on first hearing the story, listeners will nod politely–if a bit quizzically–before tucking the tale into their pocket and going on their way. They may even forget they have it until life does what it loves to do–takes a sharp turn, leading them down a road they had never intended to travel. As my father used to say, "People make plans and God laughs." It is there, in the echo of God's laughter, they will recall the tale, pondering the truth of it.

Having told the story so often to others, it's no surprise that it was the very tale I told myself on that day, several years ago, when I awoke in a hospital room to discover I could no longer speak. I had lost my voice. A Chinese story with a Jewish moral, it is the tale of a lost horse–

Long ago, in a village in China, there lived a man who owned a magnificent horse. So beautiful was this horse that people came from miles around just to admire it, telling him he was blessed to own such a horse.

"Who knows?," he said. "What seems like a blessing may be a curse."

One day, the horse ran off. People came to say how sorry they were for his bad luck.

"Perhaps," he said. "But what seems like a curse may be a blessing."

Some weeks later, the horse returned, followed by twenty-one wild horses. By the law of the land, they became his property. He was rich with horses. His neighbors came to congratulate him. "Truly," they said, "you have been blessed."

"Perhaps. But what seems like a blessing may be a curse."

Shortly after that his son tried to ride one of the wild horses. He was thrown from it and broke his leg. Surely, his neighbors said, he had been cursed.

"Perhaps," he said. "But what seems like a curse may be a blessing."

A week later, the king came through that village, drafting every able-bodied young man for a horrible war against the people of the north. Everyone who went from that village was killed. Only that man's son survived, because of his broken leg. To this day, in that village, they say, "What seems like a blessing may be a curse. What seems like a curse may be a blessing."

Just how this miracle happens—of curses turning to blessings—I cannot say, for it is different each time. But I do know it is something we make happen, through faith, love, and compassion. And when it does, we are left with a story.

Joel ben Izzy is a professional storyteller and author. His most recent book, *The Beggar King and the Secret of Happiness* (Algonquin Books, 2003), recounts a journey that began for Joel when he lost his voice after surgery. It includes the stories that helped him heal and the blessings he found along the way to recovery. For more information about Joel's travels and writing, visit his website, www.storypage.com.

Liberated by the Stones
Robin Kramer

As a female middle child with stubborn brothers on either side, I have long used words as my peacemaking weapons. As an adult, I've found that such an arsenal also comes in handy as a mother to three omniscient young men. Language is a precious resource for my community-building work as well as for occasional speechwriting.

This affection for words came embedded in my DNA: mine is a family of avid readers, a Scrabble-playing bunch with a zest for Ogden Nash. We take words seriously, having learned from an early age that the sticks-and-stones-breaking-bones-but-words-not-hurting shtick is a canard. Taking a thousand pages of admonitions from my social worker mother, my family also takes care not to gossip, convinced of its ugly capacity to destroy.

So when my mother died several months ago, it was disconcerting to discover how useless words are amidst the shuddering immediacy of death and grief. During the first month after her death, even as I assumed my usual role as good listener and shoulder, I found books, always my trusted friends in the past, to be unreliable. Poetry? Impenetrable. The guide to mourners' rituals that was meant to help? Preachy. Or this: I found I could not say, "I lost my mother," for "lost" was a word dodge, as though I had misplaced her. Or this: the *shiva minyan* seemed to be an unending series of Thou-words strung together without conveying meaning, like stacks of failed necklaces. Or this: I agreed with my friend Abby, whom I visited recently during *shiva* for her beloved sister, when she told me that "people try to be helpful, but they say really stupid things." I had special trouble with the whispered stories that were shared with me of the death of other peoples' parents or children or acquaintances. It seemed to me a bizarre form of one-upmanship. Or this: in searching for some gentle wisdom amidst the words of Kaddish, I found instead shadows and the cadence of a tired march.

Writing a eulogy for my mom was helpful. In searching for the right words, I had conversations with myself, weeping, then laughing. These were long spiritual moments tapped out on a computer keyboard, connecting me to my mother, even though on her last golden autumn morning, words eluded her.

What spoke volumes were the hugs from my boys, husband, dad, and extended family, and the quiet supportive presence of our closest friends, who journeyed from far away to be with us. What spoke to me were my dreams, cradled with gorgeous wordless melody during the entire *shiva* period.

The most enduring message I received came a month later, from a silent wall of rock and crumpled paper, when I stood at the Kotel in Jerusalem. In the decade before that trip, I had visited the ancient Temple's western wall and plaza several times. During each of these prior visits, I anticipated a radiant transformation, but it never burst forth. This time, my expectations were muted. It was a Friday afternoon. I bent forward, my forehead touching the Wall. At once, its ancient stones—heated by amber slants of sun—drew me nearer, into my mother's kind presence, sparking in me a flash flood of tears. The words of the Kaddish seemed to rise up to stroke my hair.

I was, and remain, embraced and liberated by that moment. The stones of the Kotel were a warm reminder that both words and silence are ours to use and hold and share—and to hear, when we can.

Robin Kramer, Senior Director of The Broad Foundation, also serves on the boards of Temple Israel of Hollywood, the Breed Street Shul Project, Pitzer College, the Safed Foundation, the Daniel Pearl Foundation, Reboot, and the Campaign for College Opportunity. She lives with her family in Los Angeles.

Forgiving Those Genes

Simkha Y. Weintraub

Genes, my genes, what hath thou wrought?

I know that my diabetes is "heavily genetic." Same with the thyroid problems, no doubt. And truth be told, if I wanted to, I could list acne, premature graying, and a few other irritating challenges, too. Looking into the proverbial crystal ball, I might anticipate heart disease, colon cancer, Alzheimer's, Parkinson's, and more, on this, my ledger of genetic burdens, contingencies, debits, and insults.

But then that's not fair to you, genes of mine! For I have also drawn on you, quite heavily, for some remarkable treasures–familial love, Jewish *n'shamah* (soul), a tendency to hope, a quirky sense of humor, substantial mental flexibility and patience, general adaptability, and so much more. Why impugn my gene package by highlighting only certain elements? Unfair to you–and unhelpful to me.

Back to the diabetes. My mediocre pancreas links me to my paternal grandmother, who lived with diabetes for the second 49 of her 98 years, may she rest in peace. Sure, it influenced her life and those of care-taking family members, but so did her sweetness, her devotion, her soft cheeks and audible, inhaling kisses, her worn book of Psalms and stories of the Vilna Gaon, her patched linens and sturdy love of family, God, and people.

When I look at the whole picture, the big picture, which isn't often enough, I surely come out way ahead in the trade-off.

That's my prayer, to look at the whole picture. Thank you, God, for giving me these genes– Your explanation will follow someday, I hope.

Rabbi Simkha Y. Weintraub, CSW, serves as Rabbinic Director of the New York Jewish Healing Center and the National Center for Jewish Healing, at the Jewish Board of Family and Children's Services in New York City. He is the editor of *Healing of Soul, Healing of Body* (Jewish Lights, 1994) and *Guide Me Along the Way: A Jewish Spiritual Companion for Surgery* (NCJH, 2002).

Final Search
Rami Shapiro

The air in the room was thick and damp. No one spoke, yet it wasn't silent, either: monitors beeped, mother wept, dad's rubber soles squeaked against the dull pale-green linoleum floor as he traced a path from Gary's bed to the closed door and back to the bed again. Periodically a nurse walked into the room, checked the IV dripping into Gary's arm, and smiled professionally at his parents.

Gary was born with a rare disease that began to consume him from birth. He was expected to die before becoming bar mitzvah. That was three years ago. Today he would die a man.

As his disease entered its final months, Gary developed an acute interest in reincarnation. He believed he was paying off a karmic debt, and that he would be reborn healthy and debt-free. His mom and dad rejected the idea; his aunt and uncle embraced it. Gary must be an evil soul, they reasoned, otherwise a good God would never punish him this way. To protect themselves and their children, they shunned Gary and his parents. Gary was cut off from his cousins and fell into a deep depression.

That was when his parents called me. I was Miami's 'Zen Rabbi.' I taught meditation and wrote about the spiritual dimensions of death and dying. Would I come and speak with Gary, they asked me?

Gary and I met once each week during the final months of his life. We began each session with meditation. I taught him to use the Hebrew mantra *Shema Yisrael Adonai Eloheinu Adonai Echad* (Listen, Israel: the One we call God is Oneness Itself). Breathe in "Shema;" breathe out "Yisrael;" breathe in "Adonai;" breathe out "Eloheinu;" breathe in "Adonai;" breathe out "Echad."

After twenty minutes of silence, we'd read a bit from sacred scripture: Psalms, the Bhagavad-Gita, the Gospel of Thomas. And then we talked.

In time, Gary was no longer troubled by karma. Reality was reality. Each moment arises and we must deal with it justly and with compassion. Karma was all about asking "Why?" and there is no "why." There is only this moment. So Gary and I learned to sit in silence. We learned not to ask "why." We learned how to live. He learned how to die.

And then he woke up. He had been in a coma for most of the day, and now he was pushing himself upright and leaning against the metal headrest of his hospital bed. His eyes glistened; his smile was huge, and he looked at each of us slowly in turn. He said softly: "I found it." Then he died.

The monitors whistled the fact and nurses came rushing in. "Gary's gone," one nurse said to the blank wall just above Gary's mother's head.

"Where did he go?" she said to me.

"Nowhere to go," I said.

"He's OK now, isn't he?" she said.

"He found it," I said.

"And he came back to tell us he found it and that he's OK," Gary's father said.

"And so are we," I said.

We all sat on the bed, hugging Gary and each other. And we cried.

Rabbi Rami M. Shapiro is an award-winning poet, teacher, and essayist, and his liturgies are used in prayer services throughout North America. A congregational rabbi for 20 years, Shapiro has been strongly influenced by Buddhist teachings and Kabbalah. He is president of the One River Foundation for the Study of the World's Religions. He's the author of numerous books, including *Proverbs: The Wisdom of Solomon* (Harmony/Bell Tower, 2001) and *Hasidic Tales, Annotated and Explained* (Skylight, 2003). His foundation, Simply Jewish (www.SimplyJewish.com), explores the experience and expression of Judaism in the 21st century.

Breaking the Matza
Amichai Lau-Lavie

We broke up the day before Purim. A full moon later, I was not in the mood for a joyous Passover Seder. But the spring air was clear, the moon was full, and so we gathered around a beautiful fragrant table laden with the ritual objects of the Seder. With great pomp and a flourish, we removed the embroidered cover, revealing the three matzot. Of these, the middle one was removed and then broken in two, one half quickly hidden, the other half, remaining alone on the plate, broken, waiting to be reunited with the other half. I watched this familiar ritual with new awe, suddenly remembering a saying from the Kotzker Rebbe, a Chasidic Master: "There is nothing more whole than a broken heart." Silently, I sanctified my brokenness.

A broken matza on a Seder plate: They say this 'break up' comes to balance joy and sorrow on our road to personal freedom—the inevitable two sides of life. Some say the two halves represent this world and the world to come, the revealed and the hidden. Or maybe they signify the broken tablets. Or the brokenness of our hearts. The ritual is ancient, its roots have been forgotten, but its visceral intensity and its necessity have not.

It's so hard to safely mark the difficult places, the sadness of soul, the simple pain of a broken heart. I find solace in myth and in ritual. This broken matza, on this particular Passover, comforted me, gave my mute pain voice and gesture, granted me the great blessing of the fracture, the brokenness that opens the door to new possibilities.

I sang a different freedom song at the table that night, a prayer by Sinead O'Connor:

> *Thank you for breaking my heart,*
> *thank you for tearing it apart,*
> *now I've a strong, strong heart,*
> *thank you for breaking my heart*

The moon was low in the sky when I left the Seder that night, as full as a whole matza.

Amichai Lau–Lavie is an Israeli-born mythologist, storyteller, and teacher of Judaic literature. He is the founder and artistic director of Storahtelling: Jewish Ritual Theatre Revived, a unique New York-based company of young artists and educators that fuses Torah, contemporary performance art, and ritual theater. To learn more about their productions and community programs, visit their website, www.storahtelling.org.

Embracing the Broken Pieces
Kerry M. Olitzky

The word cancer has always scared me. Perhaps it's because I heard it so frequently in my home, starting at such a young age, perhaps because it had caused the death of those I loved. Nevertheless, it seemed like a regular part of our normal family conversation. And although for most of my childhood, a diagnosis of cancer did mean almost certain death, even then cancer was still combated with a typical fix-it mentality, one fostered by the physicians and others who safeguarded the health and welfare of my family. They told us quite clearly: "If something is broken, we'll fix it. Then you just go on with life." It seemed like an appropriate formula at the time.

I remember first hearing the word at the dinner table in connection with my grandfather, and then, before I even realized that the conversational spotlight had shifted, I learned that the dreaded disease had struck my mother. As I entered adulthood, I figured naively that my family had filled its "cancer quota"–and, anyway, I assumed, such sickness was reserved for older people.

At least that is what I thought until our doctor nonchalantly dropped the news that my young wife had cancer. While getting dressed to attend her grandfather's funeral, she had spotted an unusual swelling in her neck. Cancer was the last thing that crossed our minds, but after a series of tests and examinations, the diagnosis was confirmed.

Somehow we succeeded in keeping the Angel of Death at bay through surgery and medication–and extensive vigilance, something my mother had done, as well. We made lifestyle and diet changes and even tried to reorganize the stresses that accompanied our work. Everything seemed to be going according to the surgeon's protocol–a plan we followed to the letter.

Imagine our surprise when we were told that the cancer had returned, unexpectedly. We had reached that mysterious five-year survival mark, ready to celebrate that poignant anniversary with a trip to the Caribbean, yet forced to cancel only days before we were scheduled to leave. Rather than luxuriating in a beachside hotel, we had to renew a hospital routine, one we had left behind years before, a routine our doctor had promised us we would never have to know again. The surgeon told us what I had heard before, that this time he had taken care of the disease, "cut it out," and we had nothing else to worry about. We believed him when he said, "Go on; go live the rest of your lives."

And so we planned to do so. It was not easy to do when the prospect of death constantly hovered. So we secretly and silently counted down the days, the weeks, the months until we wouldn't have to worry any longer. We waited once again for the liberation that seemed to only come with time. We often felt like our ancient Israelite brethren who had desperately sought a more expedient route to the Promised Land, one that would take far fewer years. Like them, we felt enslaved. Slavery in the restricting places of Mitzrayim, of Egypt, threatened to break us. Grappling with its narrowness was bad enough, but confronting the desert of the unknown was even more frightening.

I see now that in counting down time, we also unconsciously rushed ahead our lives—and the lives of our children—in order to get past our crisis point and be free to live. But then the cancer struck again. This time, we decided the surgeon should once again cut the cancer out of my wife's body, but we decided not to cut the cancer out of our lives. We would no longer be silent about its place in our existence. It was this healing strategy that continues to provide us comfort and support.

Like our ancestors, who used the Ark to carry the broken shards of the Tablets of Moses alongside the unbroken Tablets as they made their way through the desert, we carry the shattered remnants of Sheryl's sickness along with us. This has enabled us to continue our journey forward, learning once again the wisdom of our tradition: "You have to stumble onto Torah in order to learn it." In a way we could not have anticipated, holding onto the broken pieces has allowed us to become whole once again.

Rabbi Kerry M. Olitzky, D.H.L., is the Executive Director of the Jewish Outreach Institute (www.joi.org), the only national independent organization dedicated to bringing Judaism to both interfaith families and the unaffiliated. He has written extensively on the subjects of healing and spirituality and is the author of *Twelve Jewish Steps to Recovery* and *Jewish Paths to Healing and Wholeness* (both Jewish Lights Publishing). He lives in New York.

When the Heart Breaks (a meditation)

Jan Goldstein

Your vision will become clear only when you look into your heart.
Who looks outside, dreams. Who looks inside, awakens.
-Carl Jung

Why me, I ask? Why now when life holds so much potential?

Why did it take this happening for me to become aware of these possibilities?

Elizabeth Kubler-Ross says: "People are like stained glass windows. They sparkle and shine through when the sun is out, but when the darkness sets in, their true beauty is revealed only if there is a light from within." Where is my light, I want to know?

I sit amidst the pain of this wounding time in my life, brimming with apprehension, feeling the hard shell of my heart shattering. And yet I can see that, even as my anguish flows out, my broken heart still makes space for appreciation and illumination to flow in. My light is connected to those who love me, who touch me and those I love, with the warmth of compassion and support. Its rays pierce the dark forest of my fear, imbuing me with hope.

The breath of life rushes through my lungs at this delicate moment of my life and, if I pay attention, I notice something different, something precious and quivering and real. I must pause to savor it. This breath, this single precious gift, must be shared with all who are dear to me. In this breath lies the promise of all I cherish. In this one little miracle resides the potential for my world to continue in the midst of pain.

This precious path I walk in life is not unscathed or untroubled. But like others who are challenged by illness, loss or heartbreak, I see differently. My vision is vulnerable and yet fuller somehow. If I struggle to remain open, I am finding myself awakening to the truth that I, and each of us, matter profoundly.

"The wounded deer leaps the highest," wrote Emily Dickinson. It is at this time when I am hurt that I am capable of using all the love, all the hope, and all the goodness within me. These are what can anchor me in the storm-tossed seas of my present pain.

Guilt may bare its face to me now that I am shaken by circumstances beyond my control. I think of words unsaid or deeds undone. Erma Bombeck called guilt "the gift that keeps on giving." It is not the gift I need nor will it serve any positive purpose. Rather now is the time to concentrate on what affirms living and loving: the child who takes my hand or smiles my way; the caring touch of friends, family, and strangers, the recognition that, in all the uncertainty, all that is certain shines with a greater clarity.

Theodore Roethke said, "In a dark time, the eye begins to see." Looking with my heart, I see the angels around me. Those who make me laugh, those unafraid to express love, those who give a damn. In the maelstrom of hurt, there is healing in my seeing humanity this clearly.

In my despair, as my heart weeps, I can find, as I search within, the little boy within me. He needs holding, he needs a kiss. I need to cherish him. Hold him inside of me and let him know the strength of who he has become is here and present. I want to comfort him with the knowledge that there are others who care. He is not alone. Neither am I.

Jan Goldstein is the author of *Sacred Wounds: Succeeding Because of Life's Pain* (HarperCollins, 2003) and the rabbi of Shofar Synagogue in Los Angeles. His debut novel, *The Gifts* (Hyperion, 2004), also deals with themes of depression and renewal.

Memory & Memorial

The only truly dead are those who have been forgotten.
– *Jewish Proverb*

One Survivor Remembers
Gerda Weissmann Klein

At almost every place I speak and in the many, many letters I receive, people ask me what it was like to receive the Academy Award for "One Survivor Remembers," a documentary based on my life story. People ask, "How did it feel for you, a Holocaust survivor, to be standing in Hollywood with all the stars, the blazing jewels, and the incredible gowns–all that and holding an Oscar in your hand?"

The truth is, when I stood there, amid all the hoopla and the searchlights and all the things that so many people desire, my mind turned to one terrible recollection–my memory of the death march. I remembered those bitter cold days and nights: how cold I was, how hungry, how lonely. I was holding a battered, rusty bowl in my hand and praying that when I got to the end of the line, there would be enough food left in the kettle. And if by some miracle I got to the end of the line and the ladle went deeper and deeper and brought forth a potato, I was a winner. That potato meant much more to me than the golden Oscar. The Oscar is cold, doesn't speak to me, but the embraces of my grandchildren are tender and warm. I don't want them to live in a world where a potato is more valuable than an Oscar. But, I also don't want them to live in a world where an Oscar is so important that you forget there are people who do not have a potato.

I am often asked, "How did you go on?" I had a little picture within me, which I would take out and look at as one looks at a jewel. It was a picture of an evening at home: the living room of my childhood. My father smoking his pipe and reading the evening paper. My mother working on her needlepoint. My brother and I doing our homework. My cats sprawled on the floor. I used to call it a boring evening at home. For some, Hollywood dreams and mansions may be the ultimate fulfillment, but after all I have lived through, I now see a simple evening at home with my family as the ultimate reward.

Sometimes we need to stop and think of our own lives. While there is something bound to be missing from every life, we need to see what is already there–the opportunities you are free to pursue, the things you can learn, the things you can understand, and the things that make you valuable.

Although all people can contribute to the goodness of humanity, young people are the messengers of a time I shall not see. I am confident that in their hands and through their understanding, stories like mine will never need to be retold again.

An author, speaker, and historian, Gerda Weissmann Klein has been sharing her powerful stories about surviving the Nazi Holocaust for over fifty years. A recipient of many honors, she has authored several books, including *All But My Life* (Hill & Wang, 1995), a memoir of her wartime experiences upon which the documentary *One Survivor Remembers* is based.

Celebrate the Spirit- Song of Hope and Healing
Balfour Brickner

Over thirty years ago, my daughter Elisa died in a freak accident. It was August 2, 1973, during an extended bicycle trip through France. That day, she had gone horseback riding. During the ride she fell, hit her head on a rock (protective headgear was not in widespread use in those days), and within 24 hours, she died in a local clinic in the small French town of Blois. The cause was a subdural hematoma. She was seventeen.

Elisa's body was shipped home. We buried her on the island of Martha's Vineyard, Massachusetts, where she and her two brothers had summered since their infancy. We knew the island well. We had been residents there since 1941. In those days, the island was a low-key retreat –not the high-end resort it has become. It was an open and informal place, with easy access to every beach, some of which practiced a 'swimsuit optional' policy.

I bought land in a part of the Vineyard called Menemsha, and in the late fifties, we built a home on a hill overlooking Menemsha Pond and Vineyard Sound. It was a magnificent place in which to raise our three kids, who truly lived as "free range chickens." On any particular day they went with the wind, followed the water: swimming, sailing, fishing, boating, water skiing. Life was easy, clean, and simple. Elisa loved it there. She rests quietly now in the cemetery created and preserved by the island's Jewish community. Clearly, Elisa is in the right place.

How do we as parents face and deal with the death of a child? Children should survive parents, not leave them behind to grieve. When Elisa died, I discovered some important truths. First, talking about her–what happened to her, her life, her loves–helped me, and to this day, it helps. Shivah, the seven-day mourning period that we spend at home, is a marvelous therapeutic institution. People visit and even though the talk may drain and exhaust the mourners, it also lovingly cleanses them and provides relief. At Shivah's end, I found I could better cope with what happened. Nothing was left "bottled up inside." We had wept and laughed out every corner of every emotion. I was ready to go back to the business of trying to live without my daughter's physical presence. A sensible ritual, Shivah shouldn't be bypassed or truncated, lest mourners miss its purgative value.

I know Elisa's death was an accident. I draw no demonic or divine conclusions from what happened. God is not punitive, and was neither testing nor punishing us with her death.

I do not ask why this happened to me, to us. I know why, and I neither curse God because of it, nor blame anyone for what happened. Far from feeling robbed, we appreciate Elisa's presence in our midst as the great, brief gift it was. Elisa was a budding poet and writer. After her death, we read through her essays, poetry, and prose observations, getting back a part of the life that death had stolen from us. From these bits and scraps we learned much about her private side that we hadn't known and might never have known were she still alive. New doors to her mind opened for us.

During those carefree Vineyard summers, our daughter spent many happy hours at the wonderful community library in Chilmark, around the corner from our summer home. Now it houses the Elisa Brickner Poetry Corner, along with one of the largest poetry collections held by any private library in the State of Massachusetts. Is it a community library or a private library? It's referred to as both. We also created the annual Elisa Brickner Poetry Contest, in which over 35 young writers have their work professionally judged. Every summer, on an August afternoon, the winners give a public reading of their work. They're also awarded cash prizes. Their poems are kept in a volume on permanent display in the poetry corner. Both the contest and the poetry corner perpetuate our daughter's memory.

Elisa lives. The reality of her life extends beyond space and continues. Her energy cannot be destroyed. Today we gain access to her through commemoration and memory, the only tools we have or need to keep her alive. What of when we die? I believe in a divine economy that wastes nothing. After our death, when our memory of Elisa is no longer operative, I would like to think that this force we call divinity will find some way to continue her memory, as a part of the great cosmos some of us call eternity.

Balfour Brickner is the Senior Rabbi Emeritus of Stephen Wise Free Synagogue, New York, NY.

The Life of Memory

Eric Weiss

Robert's wife had died, and he couldn't sleep. His friends suggested he take sleeping pills. In a moment of quiet reflection, I asked him which side of the bed he was sleeping on.

"I'm sleeping on my own side," he said.

"What is on your wife's side?" I asked.

"Newspapers, books, anything. I try to read until I'm so exhausted I can't keep my eyes open and feel like I'm going to just collapse, but it doesn't really work. The night is the hardest time. I miss her the most then. I can't settle down, so I just lie awake, exhausted, in a state of agitation."

"Try sleeping on your wife's side of the bed."

It's purely anecdotal. There isn't any scientific research to prove it. But it seems that when their wives die, men in grief can sleep better when they sleep where their wives slept.

Sarah had lost her husband. "I can't sleep," she said. "I miss him so much at night. I can get through the day just putting one foot in front of the other, but I collapse exhausted into bed and just stare into the dark. And I just can't bring myself to clean out his things. Every time I do, I just end up holding his shirts and smelling them."

When Sarah started to sleep in her husband's t-shirt, she began to sleep through the night.

———

This sleeplessness experience is not exclusive to grieving husbands and wives. It occurs within the context of any close relationship. The truth is that all relationships continue after death. Many in grief will confide that they continue to talk to loved ones. They may hear their voices. They may even see them in their peripheral vision, only to have them disappear as they turn to meet them face-to-face. Sometimes they even smell their scent. Death may take away a body, but it cannot take away a memory, a hope for the future, a voice, a smell, a touch. Those belong to life. Death may leave us lonely, but it cannot take away a relationship. That belongs to the living, forever.

Rabbi Eric Weiss is executive director of the Bay Area Jewish Healing Center in San Francisco (www.jewishhealingcenter.org). He is formally trained in clinical pastoral education and spiritual direction.

A Boy, His Dad, and a Bike

Scott Fried

When I was a little boy, my father took me by the hand and led me outside to the curb in front of the house. There, on the street was my red Huffy bicycle with the white vinyl banana seat and the silver bell screwed onto the handlebars. When I looked at the tires, I saw that he had removed my training wheels.

He lifted me up onto the seat, steadied me as my sneakers found the grooves in the shiny metal pedals and began to push the bike. I remember falling off balance only a few times. With his left hand firmly gripping on the handlebars and his right hand glued to the back of my seat, my father ran alongside me and pushed me up the street.

I remember that boy. That boy alone with his dad. I remember feeling emboldened by the smooth, newly tarred blacktop under my wheels and the dip in the center of the road, and encouraged by the smile in his voice, the scent of his closeness.

When I reached the top of the street, I noticed he was gone. Mid-journey, mid-glee, he had let go of the handlebars and stood by, watching me finish the ride alone.

"Why did you let go?" I screamed down to him, climbing off the bike and furiously searching for the kickstand. "I need you here. I need you to hold me up."

He just waved at me and smiled. "You did it yourself," he yelled back. "You can do it on your own now. I trust you."

Years later, outside his hospital room, I stood next to my mother as she cried. "I don't have my friend anymore. I miss him already."

I entered his room and leaned in over his bed. "It doesn't look good, does it?" he asked me.

I squeezed his hand and said, "No Dad, it doesn't. It doesn't look good."

In an instant I was that boy again. That boy alone with his dad. In telling him the truth, I hoped that I had given him permission to look forward. A chance to look with incredible love and gratitude upon his life, to appreciate and value it, to feel for a moment fully alive and present, to make it to the top of the street, emboldened by the dip in the center of the road, the smile in my voice, the scent of my closeness.

He squeezed my hand. "Scotty," he said. "Oh Scotty."

My mom walked into the room and wept into her sleeve. The patient in the next bed made distracting noises. Soon, my brothers and sister were gathered around his bed. We hovered as he looked off into the distance. We talked about life insurance, the files in the left-hand side drawer, the house. He stared some more. He told us he loved us. Then he went to sleep.

––––––––––

A week after my father died my mother emptied all the food from the refrigerator, sat at the kitchen table and wept. "Mama...mama...why didn't you answer my prayers?" she cried. "Mama...mama...what am I going to do now?"

In keeping with our tradition, as a way of ending Shivah, the weeklong period of mourning after the funeral, my family assembled for a ceremonial walk around the block. The leaves, already surrendering to sorrow, gathered at our feet. The sun, already abdicating its place in the sky, settled on our backs. The season of change had begun.

When we reached the top of the street, I looked back for a second, remembering my father's words, and turned the corner.

Scott Fried is a teen health educator and motivational speaker who has been living with HIV since 1987. He is the author of two books, *If I Grow Up: Talking with Teens about AIDS, Love and Staying Alive,* (Scott Fried, 1997) and *My Invisible Kingdom: Letters from the Secret Lives of Teens.* His website is www.scottfried.com.

Openness to Discovery

This is one of the goals of the Jewish way of living: to experience commonplace deeds as spiritual adventures, to feel the hidden love and wisdom in all things.
– *Rabbi Abraham Joshua Heschel*

Wrestling With the Angel
Rachel Naomi Remen

Sometimes a wound is the place where we encounter life for the first time, where we come to know its power and its ways. Wounded, we may find a wisdom that will enable us to live better than any knowledge and may glimpse a view of ourselves and of life which is both true and unexpected.

Almost the last story that my grandfather told me was about a man called Jacob who had been attacked in the night as he slept alone by the banks of a river. He had been travelling and when he had stopped to make his meal and settle down to sleep, the place had seemed safe enough. But it was not so. He awakened to find himself gripped by muscular arms and pinned to the ground. It was so dark that he could not see his enemy but he could feel his power. Gathering all of his strength, he began to struggle to be free.

"Was it a nightmare, Grandpa?" I said hopefully. I often suffered from nightmares back then and had to sleep with a night-light on. I moved closer to my grandfather and took his hand. "No, Neshume-le," he answered, "it was quite real but it happened a long time ago. Jacob could hear his attacker's breath, he could feel the cloth of his garments, he could even smell him. Jacob was a very strong man, but even using all of his strength he could not free himself and he could not pin his enemy down either. They were evenly matched and they rolled on the ground and struggled fiercely."

"How long did they struggle, Grandpa?" I asked with some anxiety.

"A long, long time, Neshume-le," he replied, "but the darkness does not last forever. Eventually it was dawn and as the light came, Jacob saw that he had been wrestling with an angel." I was astonished. "A real angel, Grandpa?" I said, "with wings?"

"Yes, Neshume-le," he told me, "a strong young man with wings. With the coming of the light, the angel let go of Jacob and tried to leave but Jacob held him fast. 'Let me go,' the angel told Jacob, 'The Light has come.' But Jacob said 'I will not let you go until you bless me.' The angel struggled hard for he wanted badly to escape but Jacob held him close. And so the angel gave him his blessing."

I was very relieved. "Did he leave then, Grandpa? Is that the end?" I asked. "Yes," my grandfather said, "but Jacob's leg was hurt in the struggle. Before the angel left he touched him on the place where he was hurt." This was something I could understand, often my mother did this too. "To help it get better, Grandpa?" I asked. But my grandfather shook his head. "I do not think so, Neshume-le. He touches it to remind Jacob of it. He will carry it all of his life. It is his place of remembering."

I was very puzzled by this story. How could it be that one might confuse an angel with an enemy? But grandfather said this was the sort of thing that happened all the time. "Even so," said my grandfather, "it is not the most important part of the story. The most important part of the story is that everything has its blessing."

In the year before he died, my grandfather told me this story several times. Eight or nine years afterwards, in the middle of the night, the disease I have lived with for more than forty-five years declared itself in the most dramatic way imaginable. I had a massive internal hemorrhage. There was no warning at all. I was in coma and hospitalized for months. The darkness and struggle lasted for many years afterwards.

Looking back on it, I have wondered if my grandfather, old and close to the time of his death, had not left me with this story as a compass. It is a puzzling story, a story about the nature of blessings and the nature of enemies. How tempting to let the enemy go and flee. To put the struggle behind you as quickly as possible and get on with your life. Life might be easier then but far less genuine. Perhaps the wisdom lies in engaging the life you have been given as fully and courageously as possible and not letting go until you find the unknown blessing that is in everything.

Rachel Naomi Remen, MD, is co-founder and medical director of the Commonweal Cancer Help Program and Founder and Director of the Institute for the Study of Health and Illness (ISHI) at Commonweal, which trains health professionals who serve people with life-threatening illnesses, using a more relationship-centered approach to the practice and teaching of medicine.

My 26.2-Mile Healing Ritual
Elaine Zecher

By its nature, ritual moves us from one point to another, signifying a change. A bride and groom become spouses. Lighted candles transform a Friday moment into Shabbat. Ritual happens in stages, as does ritual time, past turning to present, becoming future.

When I decided to run in the 2004 New York City Marathon, I had no intention of performing any ritual. I only hoped to finish. As the Yiddish saying goes, "We plan; God laughs." The Holy One had bigger plans for me.

Years before, I'd wondered, with all cancer treatments completed, my "cure" decreed, and my ordinary life resumed, how I'd know if I was healed.

After cancer's mauling of a now-transformed body, how would true healing begin? The *Mi Sheberach* seeks a "whole" healing, *a refuah shleimah*, of body and soul, but our tradition knows healing takes work. It discounts quick fixes. Regardless of disease or treatment, we may still feel anguish. Memories of pain, anxiety, and fear may never leave us. We may pray for healing, yet not feel healed.

Amid such darkness, we can still cling to others' generosity of spirit, revel in our body's capacity to renew and rejuvenate itself, and augment the reservoir of wisdom life brings us. All these actions can lead to healing, but I found a more direct route: crossing the 26.2-mile marker in Central Park.

THE BEGINNING: 37,000 of us converge on Staten Island, stretching, hydrating, gathering strength for our task. After 18 weeks' training, I was counting on my body to perform for me. We had worked hard together. Three years earlier, inexplicably, it had failed me. How could my life of exercise and (candy addiction aside) healthy eating have allowed a tumor to grow within my flesh?

I had to learn what the words of *Adon Olam* teach: *beyado afkeed ruchi*, "In God's hand, I place my soul." I could not control everything, even less a serious disease. Thanks to modern medicine, skilled doctors, and a loving circle of family and friends, I survived. It was time to get back into shape. How about running a marathon? I enter unknown territory, amid the throngs and cross the START line. The ritual begins.

THE MIDDLE: Somewhere along the way, past and present merge. My training, my dark days of pain, and my hope of surviving and thriving have all combined to bring me here. Between miles 16 and 17, the moment is suddenly transformed. As I run the 59th Street bridge, every sense comes alive: the feel of the wind swishing, the sound of running shoes thumping on pavement, the breathtaking sight of Manhattan, the taste of tangy Gatorade. I feel centered, alive again. In my cancer years, a part of me had died, extinguishing some magic untraceable spark inside of me. As I move from that silent bridge to First Avenue's roaring crowds, I feel like I have been returned to life. At mile 17, the culmination: my husband and three children appear, waving me on, affirming my reason for living. I see friends from the congregation holding up a sign saying, "*Lech Lecha*, Rabbi," the same words (minus the "Rabbi") God had addressed to Abraham, telling him to go the distance, to finish the journey from Haran through Ur, into Canaan, the finish line.

THE FINISH LINE: I finish in front of over 8,000 people. Even if 29,000 people have crossed before me, I remain satisfied. In the category of female rabbis over 40, I am certain I've won first place.

To be healed might mean *shleimut*, from *shaleim*, meaning complete or whole. For me, it means *briut*, often translated as healthy, but sharing a root with the word for create. Joining with God as an active partner in the work of creation embodies the essence of healing. Unwittingly, I had crafted my own healing ritual that day on the streets of New York; I relish it now as I move into the future—healthy, happy, and transformed.

Rabbi Elaine Zecher was ordained in 1988. She has been a rabbi at Temple Israel in Boston since 1990, where she has been instrumental in developing programs designed to enhance the spiritual life and community ties of the congregation, including The Women's Study Groups, Service for the Healing of the Soul, Women's Kallah and Learner's Minyan. She grew up in Pennsylvania and is a graduate of Brandeis University.

Crossing the Sea

Phil Warmflash

The Egyptians were coming fast on our heels. Ahead of us the waves of the Sea of Reeds tossed and churned. All around we heard people crying and screaming, and then Nachshon walked into the sea. The water got deeper around him until he was almost covered and then, miraculously, the sea split!

That is one version of the story, but I prefer a midrash by Michael Cohen. In this version, Nachshon did not walk bravely into the sea. Instead, Nachshon was pushed. He was forced in, or maybe he even slipped. But somehow, Nachshon involuntarily went in and found himself treading water, trying to stay afloat. Then, miraculously–perhaps because he was aided by others who waded in after him–Nachshon moved forward through the water, causing the sea to part.

That is the Nachshon that I know, the Nachshon in whose place I have stood. That is the Nachshon who came not only out of *Mitzrayim*, (Egypt), but who also came out of *Meytzarim*, out of the narrow, constricted, dark place…a place where it's hard to imagine ever seeing light again. That's the place I was in after my daughter, Jordana, was born and I knew something was wrong. Month after month, at each phase of her development, I noticed she didn't do what the books said she should be doing. When she was seven months old, my fears were confirmed. Jordana was diagnosed with moderate to severe cerebral palsy. Nothing, not even months of speculation, could prepare my wife and me for those words. We were unable to regard ourselves as "special needs" parents, with a "special needs" child. This was not who we were supposed to be. With that diagnosis, we had slipped and suddenly, we were in the middle of the sea, calling out to God in anger, looking inward at ourselves and thinking about all of the things that we would never be able to do as a family because of this child.

But slowly, and in ways I could never have imagined, things began to change. I called a physical therapist. My wife bought books. We began to find strengths we didn't know we had. Our lives moved forward. At a certain point we went from having a child with cerebral palsy to having a daughter named Jordana, and just as we would have to deal with issues with our other children, we would have to deal with her issues. It was not the reality we anticipated, but it was our reality, and it was not going to overwhelm us. Like Nachshon, we would somehow find ourselves reaching the other shore.

These "Nachshon moments" are moments of transcendence, when the power that is deep within us links to a power greater than ourselves and gradually, imperceptibly, we are redeemed. I think about Nachshon moments when I am praying and come to *Mi Chamocha*. This prayer, traditionally recited twice each day, celebrates the moment of redemption par excellence, the Exodus. But when I say it, I think not only about a historic event, but also about those challenges that at first seemed insurmountable, the ones that threatened to tear the very fabric of life.

The Nachson experience is in everyday life the *Mi Chamocha* experience. I have come through the narrow place and have reached the other side.

Rabbi Philip Warmflash is the Executive Director of the Jewish Outreach Partnership of Greater Philadelphia and is on the faculty of the Reconstructionist Rabbinical College, the University of Pennsylvania's Penn Literacy Network, and the Whizin Institute. He and his wife Amy have three wonderful daughters, Ariel, Jordana, and Mira.

Final Shtick
Wendy Mogel

Bubbles, an 83-year-old friend of my daughter's, was an elementary school secretary all her life. Her vanity lay in her spelling ability. In the days before she died, she couldn't name the President or the day of the week, but she continued to spell with great verve. Her word of choice was the last in any sentence she heard. A visitor might say, "Bubbles, you're looking wonderful!" and she would plow ahead, spelling-bee style:

"Wonderful, w-o-n-d-e-r-f-u-l, wonderful."

Over time her family came to find her spelling habit annoying, but Bubbles was undaunted. She knew how to spell, she loved to spell, and she was going to spell.

My ninety-year-old father-in-law, Mel, looks at the sandwich in front of him and asks agreeably, "What do I do with this?" My husband explains. Mel eats, then looks at the second half of the sandwich and asks, "What do I do with this?" Clearly his short-term memory does not hold. But another quality does.

Admitted to the hospital after a 2 a.m. fall in the bathroom, Mel spends four hours in the ER. Eventually he is assigned a room. As two female attendants are slipping him from gurney to bed he looks directly at them, twinkles and asks, "You're not going to take advantage of me now, are you?"

When my husband comes to visit the next day Mel asks, "Who are you?"

"I'm your son, Michael."

Mel replies, "Doesn't surprise me!"

Mel had been a professional comedy writer. Now, he is fairly deaf and generally silent, but when he speaks, everything he says is funny. Although he appreciates our laughter, he isn't playing to an audience so as much as continuing a lifelong, wry, daily conversation with himself.

We know that charm is not always a central trait of the very old or dying. When family members lose the ability to imagine another's feelings they can become angry, blunt, or cruel. The dying can leave us long before they are gone. A friend told me that his devoted mother held his dying father's hand. The man looked his wife straight in the face and said, "I prefer the caregiver."

But some who have lost memory and other skills gain something of great value. Our world is speedy, complex, and nervous. We have layered and competing responsibilities and priorities that confuse and exhaust us. We ruminate about the past and fret over the future. We seek variety and stimulation. But to Bubbles and Mel, life is simple. Hear a word: spell it. Find yourself in the ER: flirt with the orderlies. Everything is boiled down to the basics.

Jewish tradition stipulates that it is best to die reciting the *Shema*. Ideally everyone would have the same thought and use the same words in his or her final moments. In remembering beloved family members, most of us don't recall a prayer but hold on to deathbed words as anecdote instead. We can think of these words both as a final punchline and as a vivid emblem of their personality, an ongoing part of their legend, a memory of the person that will endure. Treasured in this way a final utterance is holy, because it is a distilled essence even if the words are secular rather than religious.

Apparently, the great Jewish sage, Oscar Wilde, is also said to have focused on essentials just before he died. His parting words? "Either this wallpaper goes or I do."

 "Wallpaper, w-a-l-l-p-a-p-e-r, wallpaper."

Dr. Wendy Mogel (www.wendymogel.com) is a clinical psychologist and the author of *The Blessing of a Skinned Knee* (Penguin, 2001). She is currently writing a book about the effect of pressure and privilege on adolescents.

Up

Ellen Schecter

The following is an excerpt from Schecter's memoir, *Fierce Joy*,
which first appeared in *Ducts*, a webzine of personal stories.

I clawed my way up toward healing from way underground, so far down that the sky was just a faint, faraway polka dot of light. During that time, when I slogged along the streets of Manhattan, ferociously unhappy, I often felt more kinship with trees than with the strangers who jostled me aside. The trees neither ignored nor pitied me; they simply showed me, in elegant silence, how to survive: Keep silent. Be strong. Withstand.

One breed of tree spoke most frankly to me–those scrappy, scrawny survivors, weeds really, that try hard to become trees. You've seen them. They rise up out of the corners in trashy lots. Tough as copper pipe, they fight their way sunward from dirty footholds in storm sewers or subway shafts. Their muscular gray trunks twist and climb even murky light. They insinuate themselves under shingles and roof tiles, then signal the sky like raggedy green flags: here I am, I made it. I once lived with one of those trees: it climbed inside a rusty water-spout all the way from the basement, up to my fourth-floor window before it burst out into the sunlight like a leafy green umbrella. They don't quit, those weed-trees, and that's what they told me: Don't quit. Keep reaching. Up.

I always thought of them as "ironwood trees." But a friend recently told me they're actually called ailanthus–"the tree of heaven."

Yet, it's not their name that matters; it's how they live, what they show about healing. They seek light no matter how far underground they start. They sprout in the harshest spots, yet flourish. They clothe themselves in beauty through the simplest miracles of sun and rain. They find sustenance almost anywhere. You can hack them off at the roots and they spring up again and again, because they simply refuse to die.

I look at those trees and push up toward the light with a will as adamant as iron.

Ellen Schecter has published 24 books for children, including *The Family Haggadah* (Viking Children's Books, 1999), and written multi-award-winning television for children and families including *The Magic Schoolbus* and *Reading Rainbow* for PBS, *Allegra's Window* and *Pinwheel* for Nickleodeon. Her essays appear in print and on the Web. To read more of *Fierce Joy*, visit www.ducts.org.

Just a Broken Ankle

Elliot N. Dorff

From the very first time we met, Marlynn and I enjoyed walking together. Every night during college, after the library closed at 11 p.m., I would meet her and we would walk for an hour or so, holding hands and talking. Even after we got married and had a family, we'd take walks with the children after dinner, whether they wanted to or not. More recently, we've taken hikes together when we could.

On one of those Sunday hikes, in a local park during a beautiful January in Southern California, I slipped and broke my ankle. I had never broken anything before, and so the physical and psychological trauma was immense. I couldn't walk, so I had to be carried out of the park on a stretcher by six men, put onto the bed of a truck, and driven to a more accessible spot where an ambulance could reach me. At the hospital, the doctor told me that I had two choices: he could try to set my leg, but with no guarantees and a minimum six months' recovery, or he could do surgery the next day, and have me walking within about six weeks. I chose the latter. This doesn't seem like a standard run-of-the-mill broken ankle, does it?

That choice meant major surgery, another first for me. Once the surgery was over, it also meant depending on a wheelchair or crutches to get around. That made simple things like going to the bathroom a real chore, and my wife had to help me with showering. Fortunately, the classes I was scheduled to teach didn't begin until two weeks after surgery but once they did, I had to teach seated–much too passive an approach for me–and I was dependent on students to drive me to and from the university. I also had to cancel a few lectures that I had promised to give outside Southern California.

All these consequences were, in the greater scheme of things, minor. After all, as the doctor promised, just six weeks after surgery I was indeed walking on my own, and shortly thereafter was able to use the treadmill again. Yet during my recovery period, I remember feeling terribly wounded and acutely aware of the lack of control I had over many aspects of my life. Abilities I had taken for granted since early childhood were no longer there. I was dependent on others to do things I had previously done easily on my own. My very self-perception as an adult had been called into question. Psalm 30, part of my daily ritual since I began to daven at age fifteen, became especially meaningful to me during this time: "O Lord, my God, I cried to You, and You healed me. O Lord, You brought me up from Sheol [the grave], preserved me from going down into the Pit."

Now I am embarrassed to admit the feelings I had then.   After all, it was just a broken ankle, one that I knew would fully heal, while other people have much more serious things to worry about. And yet my feelings of frustration, depression, anger, and even self-doubt were real. My situation was far from life-threatening, yet there were certainly times I felt that way, that my life was over, and that I needed God not only to heal me but to raise me from the grave.

Being incapacitated showed me two things: First, I am much more vulnerable than I ever imagined, and so I need to thank God each day sincerely—and not just mechanically or perfunctorily—for what I can do. Second, I need to understand and empathize much more strongly with people and their problems, and seek to help them when I can. I knew those things intellectually for many years. On some level, I had also felt them emotionally and acted on those feelings. But, strange as it still seems to me, I have come to feel them much more deeply because of—yes, just a broken ankle.

Rabbi Elliot Dorff is Rector and Distinguished Professor of Philosophy at the University of Judaism in Los Angeles. He is also the author of *Matters of Life and Death: A Jewish Approach to Modern Medical Ethics* (JPS, 1998); *Love Your Neighbor and Yourself: A Jewish Approach to Modern Personal Ethics* (JPS, 2003); and most recently, *To Do the Right and the Good: A Jewish Approach to Modern Social Ethics* (JPS, 2004).

Healer of Shattered Hearts: Psalm 147
Shira Milgrom

In 1920, "Mutti," our children's great-grandmother, received a beautiful crystal punchbowl as a wedding gift. It was a one-of-a-kind, hand-cut piece, later valued at ten thousand dollars. I tell you this so you should know that it wasn't just any punchbowl. Mutti, like her family for the preceding five centuries, lived in Germany.

By the late 1930's, the grip of Nazi rule began to tighten around Mutti's life, but she was reluctant to leave her country and her home. What a home it was. Mutti had overseen the construction of her beautiful, four-story home, where the wood of the walls matched the wood of the furniture. One day in 1938, Mutti's older daughter, Ruth, who was then just a teenager, had an uneasy premonition. She convinced her parents and her younger sister to leave the house. They were all housed by Christian friends who were willing to put them up. Before she herself left, Mutti pushed a large armoire into the end of a stair landing, creating behind it a false closet. She hid there the two most precious things in her life–her diary, and the crystal bowl. The date was November 9th, 1938.

That night was the infamous *Kristallnacht*, "the night of broken glass," as organized riots of Nazi Germans destroyed synagogues and Jewish-owned businesses all over Germany. By the morning of the tenth, when the rioting subsided, Ruth would still not let her family return home; the uneasy feeling hadn't left her. And indeed, unbeknownst to them, the following night their home was destroyed.

On the third morning, Ruth asked to return home by herself. As yet, the fate of their house was still unknown to them. As Ruth rounded the corner of their street on her bicycle, she saw from a distance the front door of their home lying in the middle of the street. As she pedaled closer, she saw water pouring out of the windows from each of the floors. The Nazis had stopped up all the drains, and turned on all the faucets. As she slowly climbed the stairs, she saw the family portraits that lined the staircase slashed–knives pierced through the eyes and hearts of generations of her family. But they hadn't found the diary or crystal bowl.

The crystal bowl followed Mutti and her family on their escape route, from Germany, to England, to Chicago, and finally to Los Angeles. When Mutti died in 1990, the crystal bowl passed to her first grandchild, my husband's sister Diane, who lives in Northridge, California. Diane had always loved this bowl, and treasured it not as her own, but knew that it was in her safekeeping, to preserve for all of Mutti's generations still to come.

Two years later, an earthquake hit in Los Angeles, and the epicenter was in Northridge. David, in a quirk of fate, heard about the earthquake as it was happening and got a call through to his sister before all the phone lines went down. He could hear the pictures falling from the walls, windows shattering, glass flying. It was like another *Kristallnacht*. And Diane was hysterical. "Mutti's bowl! Mutti's bowl!" was all she could scream. David kept saying, "You're all alright. Nothing else matters." But Mutti's bowl had fallen and broken into a thousand pieces, and Diane was inconsolable.

The city of Los Angeles began to clean up—daily, trucks circling through neighborhoods picking up the huge piles of debris stacked up outside of homes. But Diane kept the pieces of the crystal bowl. Then one night she had a dream and awoke, knowing what she needed to do. On her own, she commissioned an artist friend to make a sculpture of Mutti. After months of looking at photographs and studying videos, the sculptor molded a clay form of Mutti, and then poured fourteen bronze statues, one for each of Mutti's children, grandchildren, and great-grandchildren. When they were finished, Diane presented them to her family. Mutti is seated on a stool, with her hands in her lap. And in each statue, placed in her hands, is a piece of the crystal bowl.

Broken pieces. Shattered lives.

We can move to heal our lives no matter what, no matter how old or how young, no matter how strong or how weak, no matter at what point in our lives. An important step towards healing our lives is having faith that we are part of a whole, part of wholeness. That just because something breaks and shatters into pieces doesn't mean there's no meaning left in the shards. Broken dreams, failures, disappointments, struggles, pain, and suffering. We can take the broken pieces in our lives and create from them something new. A legacy of love that will be for the generations.

Shira Milgrom is the Rabbi of Congregation Kol Ami in White Plains, New York, and the author of numerous articles on Jewish spirituality, education, and healing. She's editor of a unique Siddur (prayer book) now used in settings across the continent and she speaks frequently on topics ranging from young leadership to aging. She and her husband, Dr. David Elcott, are the parents of four children and one daughter-in-law.

Texts, Prayer, & Ritual

If not the study of the Torah, which is my delight, if not the study of the sciences, which helps me overcome my grief, I would be lost.

– *Maimonides (Rambam)*

O Lord, Won't You Buy Me...
Paul M. Yedwab

For years I have been praying for a brand new Jaguar to appear in my driveway. Somehow, it has never worked. At the other end of the spectrum of prayer, there have been times in my life when, feeling confused and distressed, I've prayed for perspective, strength, and wisdom. Often those prayers are answered. I am not talking here about some psychological, self-help, relaxation technique type of answering; I am talking about Revelation, a Buberian I-Eternal Thou moment of divine understanding.

So I'm pretty clear about the power of worship in my own life. It is in the field of healing, however, that this question of the efficacy of prayer becomes most confusing, for healing sits right in the middle of our prayer spectrum, halfway between praying for impossible physical benefits (a Jaguar) and attainable spiritual goals (perspective). It sits at that elusive point where body, mind, and soul connect.

What do we know? We know that prayer is not a cure-all when it comes to illness. Several years ago, an eighteen-year-old boy in my congregation, handsome, athletic, brilliant, good, and always kind, died of a rare, fast-growing cancer called Ewing's Sarcoma. An entire congregation prayed fervently for Evan to be cured, but the illness was simply too strong for prayer or medicine. If prayer were a cure for cancer, I truly believe that Evan would have been spared. That is not how prayer works. On the other hand, we have all read of medical studies that seem to indicate that prayer may have a positive effect on a patient's condition. So, I pray. I say a daily *Mi Shebeirach* for those among my friends, and my congregation, who are in need of healing. I do not know the exact effect my prayers will have, but there is that point where our bodies and our minds and our souls do come together, and so I aim my prayers at that sacred intersection which is within all of us.

I should mention here that lately, I have moved beyond asking God for anything in my prayers. During the *Amidah*, I see myself as entering God's living room for a heart-to-heart chat. Even more recently, I have been thinking that perhaps I am not the author of my prayers at all. Perhaps the prayers are actually God's; they are out there. God's light is all around us, and we as worshippers are simply prisms, hoping to reflect that light back upon our world in even more beautiful colors. Will those reflected prayers help to heal me? Heal others? I do not know. But to me it feels like the answer is yes. And so, I pray.

Rabbi Paul Yedwab has served Temple Israel of West Bloomfield, Michigan, since 1986. He has published five books, including *The Alef-Bet of Blessing; Learn Hebrew Today* (UAHC, 1998), *Sex in the Texts* (UAHC, 2001), and *The God Book* (UAHC, 2002).

Pirkei Refu'ah: Maxims of Healing
Cynthia Culpeper

I.   *Eize hu ashir?*

"Why me?" People frequently inquire if I ask that question. I was a hospital nurse in San Francisco before I entered rabbinical school, and now people wonder, "Do you ever ask yourself, or ask GOD, why? While helping people in a hospital setting, why did you get AIDS?"

I think they're surprised or even disappointed when I respond that I've never even thought of asking the question. As others who struggle with illness and personal tragedy have said before me, if one were to ask such a thing, one would also have to question the good things in life, too.

In my own life, I know that in any given day, countless things could have gone wrong, could have proved fatal, even, and yet were not. Yet we don't pause at day's end to contemplate these happy twists of fate. We don't ask ourselves, "Why me? How could I be so lucky?" I don't indulge in circular meditations of "what if." I'm more interested in learning the difficult habit of feeling gratitude for what is.

When I do find myself in a reflective frame of mind, pondering my fortune in comparison to that of others, it's not to engage in self-pity or complaint. Instead, I count off how many of my friends have succumbed to this disease at such a young age, yet here I am, eight years since my diagnosis, and I'm still tickin'. I think about the people who can't possibly afford the expensive medications that I take regularly, while I have adequate health insurance. I benefit from the high-quality medical treatment that's available to me and to many other Americans. If I had smaller resources, or lived in a part of the world with fewer services, I wonder if I'd still be alive. I am so mindful of how many people with my same diagnosis have lost their jobs as a result, or have felt compelled to leave their communities, yet I live in a community that has extended its support, that understands my limitations and offers many creative opportunities for me to continue my work as a rabbi.

If anything, I find numerous occasions for me to quote from Pirkei Avot: *Ei-ze hu ashir?* (Who is rich?) *Ha-sameach b'chelko* (One who is happy with his lot).

Undeniably, I wouldn't choose this diagnosis or its accompanying burdens. Yet, when I truly think about my lot, my place in the world, I count myself as rich.

II.   *Gam Zu L'Tova , Kol ma she-ADONAI oseh, hakol l'tova*

Although I don't ask, "Why me?" I do ask, What am I supposed to learn from having AIDS? As I'm convinced there is a lesson to be learned from every experience, so too do I believe, as written in Ecclesiastes Three, that there is a purpose for everything.

Recently while in Safed, Israel, with a friend, we searched and eventually found the site of *Kever Nahum Ish Gam Zu*–the gravesite of the Talmudic figure, Nahum. He is important to me because of his epithet. Variant readings notwithstanding, the Talmud tells how, despite numerous calamities that befell him on a particular journey, he was able to acknowledge, *Gam zu l'tova* (This too, is for good). A similar type of story is told about Rabbi Akiva. After suffering from a series of mishaps on a journey, he was able to say: *Kol ma she-ADONAI oseh, hakol l'tova* (All that GOD does is for good).

Life with chronic illness is also a journey, perhaps not unlike those of these two rabbinic figures. I have experienced my own series of misfortunes. I am not yet able to read their outcome as positive. But I too believe that with each step, *gam zu l'tova*. I need to believe in a world, and in a GOD that does make sense–even if it doesn't seem so from where I stand at the moment. Even if I may not come to understand it in my lifetime. How else can anyone bear heartache and grief if not by believing that on a cosmic scale, there must be righteousness and equilibrium?

We are told that a positive attitude and belief are half the battle in fighting illness, and so I try to maintain both. I try to foster a sense of gratitude when I repeat, *Ei-ze hu ashir? Ha-sameach b'chelko*. Yet I yearn also for the time when answers will be forthcoming, when everything will indeed feel in balance. Until then, again and again, I try to affirm, *Gam zu l'tova*.

At 15, Cynthia Culpeper was a student at a Catholic high school in San Francisco with an assignment due on comparative religion. She approached the rabbi at B'nai Emunah synagogue to ask some questions. That meeting led to an insatiable curiosity about Judaism, and eventually, to a lifelong commitment. As an adult convert, she left the nursing profession to attend rabbinical school, ultimately becoming Alabama's first Conservative female rabbi in 1995. She made history again in 2000 when she traveled to Poland for the High Holy Days, becoming the first female ever to lead religious services in that country. Rabbi Culpeper lives in Birmingham, Alabama.

Healing Psalms
Jerri Chaplin

As a poetry therapist, I've observed the way written expression and healing go hand in hand. This should come as no surprise, as they have been linked throughout the ages. The Greeks revered Apollo as god of both healing and poetry. During the Civil War, Walt Whitman took poems into hospital tents. Language and expression have important roles to play in the practical task of spiritual and physical recovery. The Psalms are a powerful example. I've seen firsthand the way they provide comfort to those who are demoralized by illness, burdened by grief, or seeking faith and hope to heal their spirits.

Psalm Six

Lord, do not rebuke me in your anger;
do not punish me in your wrath.

Have pity on me, Lord, for I am weak;
heal me, Lord, for my bones are racked.
My spirit shakes with terror;
how long, O Lord, how long?

Turn, O Lord, and deliver me:
save me for your mercy's sake.

For in death no one remembers you;
and who will give you thanks in the grave?

I grow weary because of my groaning;
every night I drench my bed
and flood my couch with tears.

My eyes are wasted with grief
and worn away because of all my enemies.

Depart from me, all evildoers.
for the Lord has heard the sound of my weeping
The Lord has heard my supplication;
The Lord accepts my prayer.

All my enemies shall be confronted and quake with fear;
they shall turn back and suddenly be put to shame.

Recently I, who had never suffered more than the flu, was diagnosed with a serious auto-immune disease. I was literally numb with shock after receiving the diagnosis. I couldn't take in whole paragraphs of information. What I could manage was one line at a time. I turned to the Psalms. After nearly three weeks of anxiety, I learned I had been misdiagnosed. It was then that I was able to write my own psalm of thanksgiving:

Oh, God,
who has seen fit to redeem me,
to give me a second chance
How can I honor your mercy and goodness?
As I have learned from my fear and frailty,
as the harsh wind whipped against my fragility,
make me that strong.
Help me to be a more compassionate healer,
wiser woman, more faithful friend
as generous as your boundless oceans
as warm as your ever-returning sun.
As my voice emerges from the cave of fear
hear my song, help me ever to sing it
in praise of You who have held me in your hand

Jerri Chaplin is a certified poetry therapist in Charleston, South Carolina. A former VP of the National Association for Poetry Therapy, she is the recipient of its 1999 Outstanding Achievement Award and was the first poet in residence at the Gibbes Museum of Art.

T'Shuvah Behind the Walls
Mark Borovitz

In December of 1986, when I was thirty-five years old, I was arrested for the umpteenth time. I had been arrested so often in those years that it's impossible for me to recall the details of each incident, except that this time, something was different. I wasn't sure what it was until I reached the Van Nuys police station and was put into a holding cell. Then it hit me. Once again, I was going to be separated from my six-year old daughter, Heather, but this time it was unusually hard to bear. I had been on the run for three months before the arrest. During that time, I was already feeling the loss of not seeing her, of not holding her or talking to her. Usually, I anesthetized myself against the pain of missing her by drinking. By the time of this arrest, I was already drinking about a gallon of whiskey a day, but it couldn't alleviate the intense loneliness and sadness I felt. I missed Heather terribly.

I called my first wife and told her to pick up the money I'd had with me when I was arrested. I knew that I was going to prison and so at the very least, I wanted her to have some money. She asked me which bail bondsman to call, and I told her not to call anyone. "The man upstairs is trying to give me a message," I told her, "and I have to sit here and figure it out." During that difficult moment, I realized that the only way to deal with life was to ask God for help.

In prison, after I met the prison's Jewish chaplain, Rabbi Mel Silverman, the long process of changing and saying goodbye to my former life began. He sparked my desire to rediscover where I came from and how to get back there.

At one point, I asked the rabbi if he would give up on me. He said: "You're a Jew, one of my own; I could never let you go." I cried at that moment like I had not cried in 21 years, since the death of my father. I believed the rabbi could help me come to terms with all that I had lost in those last two decades of my life. He taught me that no guard, no inmate, no one could completely strip me of my dignity. I had done that all by myself. He taught me how to regain that dignity and respect. Once I restored it myself, no one could take it from me ever again.

With Rabbi Silverman, I learned Jewish texts, absorbing Torah in a way that changed my life. When I read the story of Jacob in particular, I knew change was possible. Jacob was a con man and a thief. He had his dark night of the soul when he was preparing to go meet with his estranged brother. Jacob decided to do *T'Shuvah* (repentance). His brother, Esau, accepted Jacob's efforts and made his return easy. Esau tried to repair the relationship. The lessons for me were clear. I had to do the work, and then life could be good.

My six-and-a-half year old daughter sent a letter to me in prison. She wrote that she hated me, because when I was in jail, part of her was in jail, too. Thinking of her words, I cried and kept changing, so that she would never have to be in prison again.

After my arrest, I dealt with the losses in my life through Torah. At my request, my brother sent me a *chumash* and a *siddur* and I continued to study. I lived through two and a half years of prison by studying and living Torah. Instead of holding me back, prison life prompted me to delve deeper into Torah and *derech eretz*, the right path. I have recovered my life thanks to God, *Baruch Dyan HaEmet* (blessed is the Judge of Truth). God opened up my eyes so that I could see that I was more than a criminal. I'm a holy soul who, through the Grace of God, the help of so many other teachers, and my daughter's love, is at last able to live as a *mensch*, an honorable person who lives among others, fully and compassionately present in the world.

Rabbi Mark Borovitz is the Senior Rabbi of Beit T'Shuvah in Los Angeles, the first Jewish Residential Recovery Center. The Center uses Judaism, the twelve-step model and psychotherapy in its treatment programs. Borovitz is also the co-author of the forthcoming *The Holy Thief* (William Morrow), an inspirational memoir based on his personal experiences. Visit www.beittshuvahla.org.

Paradoxes and Healing
David Wolpe

For thus said God who dwells on high and whose name is holy: 'I dwell on high, in holiness; Yet also with the contrite and lowly in spirit -- reviving the spirits of the lowly, reviving the hearts of the contrite' (Is. 57:15).

God is both far and near, as we are both robust and broken. God is both retribution and love, as we are both ego and fragility. All of our conceptions of God embrace paradox, for we are contradictory and confused.

When a person is in pain, there is no assurance that God's presence will be felt. The foolish bromide that "there are no atheists in foxholes"—that pain or fear guarantees faith—is clever but false. Many people emerge from difficulty still searching, and some still indifferent. We yearn for consistency but live with ambiguity.

If pain does not give certainty, it does create possibility, vulnerability. Pain encourages us to reach beyond the shell we wear to fend off the insults of everyday life. We are no longer able to behave as if everything is all right; there is the chance that our souls can probe for the One who is not only Creator, *Boreh et hakol*, but comforter *rachmana*—the merciful One.

Too often our conception of God impedes our connection to God. Since we "know" in advance what God is, we know that we cannot, or have not, felt a relationship with that God. But of course God transcends our ideas and is never what we think.

The Midrash tells us that when the Torah was given, it appeared to each individual like a mirror. God's word is dependent on each human soul. God's presence in the world is never identical to two people. Light shines off each ripple of water differently. To come to God it often helps to begin by not knowing what it is we will feel, what it is we will meet.

The Bible reminds us that "the fool says in his heart that there is no God" (Ps. 14:1). Notice —not in his head, but in his heart. That is the organ of perception. We cannot reason our way to God. When the Bible speaks about God, it is clear to emphasize God's connection to the heart: "God is close to those whose hearts are broken" (Psalm 34:19). What is it you feel when you endure a bit more than you thought possible? When for the first time you smile, after the certainty

93

that a smile would never again be part of your life? It may seem trivial to invoke God at such moments, but the Bible's first assurance is that we are created in God's image. Significant moments of human life are not trivial to the Creator of all. Are such moments in a child's life trivial to a parent?

Each morning, the daily prayer service includes the following, "And I will betroth you to Me forever, yea, I will betroth you to Me in righteousness and in justice, in loyalty and in love. And I will betroth you to Me in faithfulness, and you shall know the Lord" (Hosea 2:21). In moments both joyous and pained, one comes to God through relationships. Relationships are not straightforward. They change and confuse us, confound our expectations. But it is our relationships, if we are fortunate, that heal the wounds of our hearts, and the anguish of our souls.

David Wolpe is the Rabbi of Sinai Temple in Los Angeles, California. Called a "theologian with the heart of a poet," he has authored several bestselling books, including *Healer of Shattered Hearts: A Jewish View of God* (Penguin, 1991) and *Making Loss Matter: Creating Meaning in Difficult Times* (Riverhead, 2000).

Healing

Heal them in Heaven, O God;
Heal us on earth.

Heal us for those who died over time,
And heal us for those who died overnight;
who rose above pain,
who died with the fire of resentment in their eyes,
who died in their sleep.
Heal them all by Your still waters,
in Your Garden of Healing.
within the secure bounds of Your palatial estate
spread out beyond the eye's powers to see
the hills green and speckled wild with soothing flowers.

And heal us,
through the Shivas of life,
Heal us, O God,
through the thirty days, the year.
Teach us to remember to forget
and to remember.

- *Danny Siegel*

Healing Time

Time, of itself, does not heal all hurts.
Much remains, sometimes too much.
For some unknowable number,
time does not heal wounds.

Complain to God, Yes.
Cry, "Unjust!" "Before her time!" "Such suffering!"
But do not mutter or whine.

Pray for one moment's clarity of the Saintly Ones:
all days, every day — a gift,
all heartbeats, every one of them — a blessing.

"Never enough!" cries out our human soul.

Ask for one precious second's seeing
in the mind's eye of the Righteous.

- *Danny Siegel*

An author, poet, educator, and lecturer, Danny Siegel has traveled extensively around the country speaking to Jewish audiences about *tzedakah*, community involvement, "mitzvah work," and Jewish values. He is founder and chairman of the Ziv Tzedakah Fund (www.ziv.org).

A Sacred Scroll
Naomi Levy

Just because there are pieces inside us that have broken does not make us broken human beings. Having scars doesn't mean that we're damaged goods, irredeemable or permanently tainted. Sometimes people feel so scarred by a hurt that they have trouble seeing the larger part of themselves that is still left whole, perfect, and intact, the part that can never be broken or destroyed, no matter what pains we have endured.

I will never be the same person as I was before my father's murder. I've changed. It's a conscious and difficult effort, those times I try to remember what that Naomi was like, the one who was not hurt by life. But I also recognize that there are parts of me that have not changed at all. There is an aspect of my being that doesn't need any healing because it can never be injured or ruined; it remains and will remain constant and firm.

When I was about twelve or so, I wanted to learn how to read the Torah. All the boys in my class were reading from the Torah in preparation for their bar mitzvah ceremonies, but girls weren't permitted to join the class. I begged, pleaded, and protested, but the rabbi of my youth said, "When a girl gets her period, she's impure. If you touch the Torah when you're impure, you'll make the Torah impure." That was the end of our discussion. In short, I should have known better than to want to contaminate the Torah.

Years later, during my own rabbinic training, I learned that rabbi was wrong. It's true that Judaism views menstruation as a time of impurity. But the Torah can never receive that impurity. It is deemed so sacred by our tradition that nothing can render it impure. Nothing. Not even me.

Not even the most terrible and deliberate act of desecration can render a Torah impure. There is a horrifying account in rabbinic literature about how Titus defiled the Torah and Temple. The narrative of that event reads just like a rape scene: "The wicked Titus entered the Holy of Holies with his sword drawn. He slashed the curtain and his sword came out covered with blood....He took two prostitutes, spread out a Torah scroll beneath them, and proceeded to have sex with them on top of the altar."

Nothing has dominion over the holiness of a Torah scroll, not even its physical destruction. During the Roman persecutions in Israel, the great rabbi Hanina ben Teradion was sentenced to death for openly teaching Torah in defiance of the Roman ban. The Talmud offers this account of his execution: "They took him, wrapped him in a Torah scroll, tied vines around him, and set them on fire. They took woolen sponges soaked in water and placed them over his heart, to make sure that he would not die too quickly….His disciples cried 'Master, what do you see?' He replied, 'The parchment is burning, but the letters are soaring up to heaven.'"

Within each of us, I believe, there lies a space that is as indestructible as a sacred scroll. A holy, eternal space that can't be altered or tarnished. A space of purity and wisdom. It is in this space that we find the inner resources and the strength to rebuild our lives after tragedy. Not even death can have dominion over it. When we die, it soars upward back to God just like the letters of the Torah. Call it the soul, the life breath, the spirit. We all have access to it. It is the seat of God within each of us. Not the God of my childhood fantasies who comes to our rescue like Superman. Not the God who can prevent evil or cure disease. But the God who can heal us by being beside us in our suffering. The God who gives us strength to dream once more. The God who assures each and every one of us, You are not alone, I am with you.

A Prayer:

When I feel tainted, God, remind me that I am holy.
When I feel weak, teach me that I am strong.
When I am shattered, assure me that I can heal.
When I am weary, renew my spirit.
When I am lost, show me that You are near.

Amen

Rabbi Naomi Levy is author of the national bestseller *To Begin Again: The Journey Toward Comfort, Strength, and Faith in Difficult Times* (Knopf, 1998) and *Talking to God: Personal Prayers for Times of Joy, Sadness, Struggle and Celebration* (Knopf, 2002).

Deep Calleth Unto Deep
Sheldon Marder

"I will never forget the feeling of stepping off a cliff when the doctor told us that our newborn son had a heart defect."

So begins the story of Zachary, a mother's account of a tiny life that lasted less than a week. Melinda Ruchames ends her son's story with this report:

Pathology Report: This was a well-developed, four-day-old, white male infant who expired following surgery, an attempted repair for transposition of the great vessels [pulmonary artery and aorta were reversed, causing the circulation of unoxygenated blood].

Gross Autopsy Findings: The body is cold…there is a small amount of light brown scalp hair…the eyes are blue-gray. The penis is uncircumcised…longest finger length is 3.2 cm. Organs occupy their usual positions. Peritoneal surfaces are glistening and smooth. The testes have the normal architecture. The pituitary lies in the sella. The brain is soft. Leptomeninges are delicate.

A Mother's Addendum: "His hair was dark not light brown, like his father. He would have been circumcised on the eighth day, but we buried him that day instead. All the nurses commented on his long fingers…My heart is cold and lies in darkness. It is very delicate. I think it may be broken. My life has lost its normal architecture, and nothing will occupy its usual position ever again."

––––––––––

My life has lost its normal architecture.

It's the emotional equivalent of a house with gaping cracks, a steady leak, smashed panes, sagging beams and, most crushing of all, a small empty room. The image brings to mind a question fired ages ago at God by one of the Bible's bitterest writers, the author of Psalm 88, who asked in his grief: "Are Your wonders made known in the place of darkness?" Like the grieving mother, Melinda, that poet knew how it felt to step off a cliff and find oneself "in the lowest recesses of the Pit, in the darkest places, in the depths" (Ps. 88:13, 7).

In those places, where is the hope? Where is the healing? Where is the One who lifts up the fallen?

Years ago I came upon this cryptic but evocative statement: "Rabbi Ezekiel Bennet willed that he be buried among the infant dead." He wanted his grave to be among those visited by the most grief stricken and heartbroken of mourners. Rabbi Ezekiel, it seems, wished to attach himself to souls in search of hope and healing.

––––––––––

Formal Jewish mourning practices are not required when a newborn dies before thirty days of life. But the Talmud tells stories (in tractate Shabbat 136a) about two fathers–Rav Kahana and the son of Rav Dima–who chose to mourn their babies even when others suggested that it might be unnecessary.

There is a need. In the dark places, in the depths, there is a need that transcends the law.

Melinda describes different kinds of needs, and how Jewish ritual helped:

"The decision to have a funeral was very important to me. It validated Zachary's existence. It affirmed his life that was so precious to me…. The funeral allowed us to make a statement to ourselves, our families, and our community: this child was real to us, and we will not deny him. It established the foundation of our mourning and gave it a legitimacy….

 Having some choices helped me feel more in control over this event that had made me feel so powerless. At the same time, knowing there was some structure relieved me….of creating a format for my mourning…. It comforted me to think that mothers for centuries had mourned their children as I was mourning mine…. I was part of something bigger than myself and this tragedy that seemed to fill the whole world…. I was doing the same things, saying the same prayers that women had read for thousands of years. I felt a connection to all of those who had grieved. I knew that I was not alone…. Others had been there before me in this part of the dance of life."

––––––––––

For centuries, Bible scholars have been baffled by the mysterious words "deep calleth unto deep" in Psalm 42. Although she believes that grief will be a part of her life forever, Melinda's experience teaches us the meaning of the psalmist's poetry: the deepest wellsprings of Judaism call to us in our times of deepest need. In that call there is hope. In that call there is healing.

And where is the One who lifts up the fallen? I like to think that God, like Rabbi Ezekiel Bennet, dwells among the graves of the infant dead, of blessed memory–attaching Himself to mothers and fathers in search of solace.

Zachary was born January 4 and died January 9, 1987. His brother Benjamin was four years old at the time. Melinda Ruchames and her husband, Eric, had a third son, Nathan, on July 15, 1988. Nathan became bar mitzvah on August 25, 2001.

Rabbi Sheldon Marder provided pastoral care to the Ruchames family, led the funeral, and delivered Zachary's eulogy. Marder also had an aliyah at Nathan's bar mitzvah. He is the rabbi of the Jewish Home for the Aging in San Francisco.

Hope & Healing—A Moment of Mishnah
Bradley Shavit Artson

When the world crashes in on me, I retreat to the core of my soul. The writings of our sages are like a haven within which I find a safe space of calm, of care, and of healing. When the whirlwind of my job shakes me, when stress at home or a challenge facing my children threatens to pull me under, I sit in the quiet of my study and I open a Jewish book.

The words pull me into another place. The words remind me of my true center. The words heal me.

Embedded within the texts, among the most dry and technical concerns, I sometimes encounter an eruption of light. It breaks through the surface, shattering what had been a smothering darkness. In my life, in our sacred writings, in the innermost chambers of my soul, there I can uncover illuminating sparks that offer light, warmth, hope.

An example: In the middle of an ancient rabbinic discussion of the laws of purity and impurity, the question at hand—itself brittle and dry—is, what kind of vessels can be used to carry sacrificial material? *Mishnah Zevahim* 88a opens with a simple assertion, "The vessels for liquids sanctify liquids, and the measures for dry matter sanctify dry matter. A liquid vessel does not sanctify dry matter, nor does a dry [measure] sanctify a liquid." Dry works for dry; wet works with wet. Like to like, the way the world appears when we are despondent—bad things happen to me, good things happen to someone else. Why does it seem as if other peoples' lives are charmed?

But the Mishnah refuses to leave matters there, in the depressing trap of victimology. It isn't enough to assert that dry goes with dry and wet goes with wet. What happens when life is more complex than our sorrow and our fear might suggest? What about when something that once worked becomes broken in the course of its use? What then?

"If holy vessels were perforated yet they can be used for the same purpose as when whole, they sanctify [what is placed in them]; if not, they do not sanctify." Here the Mishnah speaks to the hole in our heart. I was once robust; I was once strong; I was once invincible. The passage of time, the weight of the tasks, and life's wounds have punctured my imperviousness. I am breaking. Does that mean I am now useless? Human garbage? No, answers the Mishnah's anonymous (hence authoritative) voice: even when broken, if we can still perform some of what we were intended for, still serve some of the role we are called to, then we still sanctify. We still have a holy mission and a purpose. We still reflect the divine image of God.

The Mishnah concludes with one last insistence: "And all these sanctify only in the holy." Whole or broken, disabled or not-yet-disabled, all are holy. The place in which we can carry each other, sanctify each other is in a place of holiness. And, for us, the place of holiness is the place in which everyone counts, a place of dignity, inclusion, and love.

A last word: After Mishnah comes Gemara. After description comes reflection. The rabbis of the Talmud (specifically the great sage Shmuel) offer a profound image of the blessing to be found amid challenge, illness, and loss: "Shmuel said: The service vessels sanctify only when *whole*. They sanctify only when *full*, and they sanctify only from their *interior*." Whether the vessels are broken or whole, whether they function still or no longer, their holiness abides in these three virtues: wholeness, fullness, and interiority.

When we are whole, not in a superficial, corporeal way, but whole in our own centeredness (in knowing who we are and what we stand for), when we are *full* (full of love for ourselves, for each other, for creation, for God), and when we shine to the world our truest self (isn't that what *interiority* is all about?), then whether we're physically broken or not, whatever our degree of function, we are able to connect to the holiness just under the surface—ours and God's—to continue to sanctify ourselves, each other, and Creation.

Rabbi Bradley Shavit Artson is the Dean of the Ziegler School of Rabbinic Studies at the University of Judaism, where he is Vice President. He is the author of *The Bedside Torah: Wisdom, Visions, & Dreams* (McGraw-Hill, 2001).

My Favorite Verse in the Whole Torah
Jack Riemer

My favorite verse in the whole Torah comes right near the beginning. Adam and Eve have two children, Cain and Abel. The two children fight. It's not clear what the fight was about. One Sage says it was about property, another says that it was about a woman. A third says it was about religion, with each one insisting, "The Holy Temple will be built on MY land." We don't know what they fought about. All we know is that one brother killed the other.

Where were the parents when this was going on? We don't know. They are somewhere off-stage–perhaps at a PTA meeting, learning how to raise children. At any rate, they come back and they find that they have lost two children–one is dead and the other is sentenced to exile. He runs away, and they never see him again.

What would you do, what would I do, if, God forbid, that happened to us, if we lost two children at one time? Listen to what they did (italics mine):

"Adam made love to his wife *again* and they had another child." Genesis 4:25

They don't forget the two children whom they have lost–no bereaved parent ever does. They mention these two in the very moment when they name this child. "She named him Seth, meaning 'God has provided me with another child in place of Abel whom Cain killed.'"

I love that sentence: Adam made love to his wife *again*. In Jewish tradition Adam is called Adam Harishon–Adam the First. But it's no big deal to be the first. He happened to be the first person created–that's just a matter of chronology. And it's no big deal to make love and to have a child when you're young–your libido makes you do that. But to love and lose and love *again*? That takes courage!

So Adam and Eve become the models for all the losers in the world, and who isn't at some time in his or her life a loser? They are the models for all those of us who love and lose and start over again. And it's a good thing that they did. If they hadn't, we would all be descended from a killer or from a victim. Now they are our uncles, and we are all descended from Seth instead.

The Midrash says that when Adam and Eve lost their two children, they did not want to make love again. Can you blame them? Does it make sense to go through nine months of pregnancy if it all ends like this? Does it make sense to make love if the end is death? The Sages say that they were overcome with nausea and disgust and despair. And so God had to implant an extra measure of desire within them, before they were willing to try again. And so it is with us.

Human resilience is, to me, the great proof of God's existence. For where else do human beings get the strength to get up off their knees and begin over again? There is no secular explanation for what Adam and Eve did, and for what so many people we all know have done ever since. For human beings to begin is easy–your libido makes you do that–but to begin over again? To be defeated by life and to start over again–this to me is one of the wonders of the world.

What would Adam and Eve say to those of us who are broken in spirit and disappointed by life? Perhaps this:

> When you love,
> Give it everything you have,
> And when you have reached your limit–
> Give it more,
> And forget the pain of it
> Because, when you face your death,
> It is only the love you have given and received
> Which will count;
> And all the rest–
> The achievements, the struggles, the fights–
> Will be forgotten
> In your reflection;
> And if you have loved well
> Then it will have been worth it,
> And the joy of it
> Will last you through the end,
> But if you have not--
> Then death will always come too soon–
> And be too terrible to face.

- *Anonymous*

Often referred to as "the rabbi's rabbi," Jack Riemer is the editor of six books of modern Jewish thought, including *Wrestling with the Angel: Jewish Insights on Death and Mourning* (Schocken, 1995). His essays and reviews appear frequently in journals both in the United States and abroad, and his prayers appear in the prayer books of the Conservative, Reform, and Reconstructionist movements.

Notes:

Write to us:

If you have stories to share about using
this book with friends or family,
or if you have your own healing story to tell,
let us know about it.
You can also write just to share
your reactions to these essays.

You can reach us at:

Craig 'n Co.

P.O. Box 6061-115

Sherman Oaks, CA. 91423

Email: info@craignco.com

Catalog

To order additional copies of *The World is a Narrow Bridge*, the *Narrow Bridge* companion CD, or any other items from our catolog, please visit our website: www.craignco.com or call 1-800-6-craig-8.

Recordings

We Were As Dreamers
New Beginnings
Moment To Moment
Makin' Music
Pennies for Your Thoughts
Yad B'Yad
Craig 'n Co.
Yad B'Yad Together
Encore
Morning 'n Night
Journey
Rock 'n Together
Heaven and Earth
Rock 'n Toontown
Voice of the Spirit
Kol Tikvah
My Jewish Discovery
Imaginit
Peeps Sing-a-Long
My Newish Jewish Discovery

Friday Night Live
Best of the Rest
One Shabbat Morning
Celebrate Hannukkah
Celebrate Shabbat
Celebrate Passover
Celebrate Kids
Celebrate Jewish Love Songs
Celebrate Peace
Celebrate Jewish Hip
Celebrate Klezmer
Celebrate Yiddish

Books

Craig Taubman Songbook
New Jewish Songs
Seven Weekends that Make a Difference
Voices of the Spirit–Inspirations and Meditations
Friday Night Live Songbook
Best of the Rest Songbook
One Shabbat Morning Songbook